# CAMBRIDGE LIBRARY COLLECTION

*Books of enduring scholarly value*

## English Men of Letters

In the 1870s, Macmillan publishers began to issue a series of books called 'English Men of Letters' – biographies of English writers by other English writers. The general editor of the series was the journalist, critic, politician, and supporter (and later biographer) of Gladstone, John Morley (1838–1923). The aim was to provide a short introduction to each subject and his works, but also that the life should illuminate the works, and vice versa. The subjects range chronologically from Chaucer to Thackeray and Dickens, and an important feature of the series is that many of the authors (Henry James on Hawthorne, Ward on Dickens) were discussing writers of the previous generation, and some (Trollope on Thackeray) had even known their subjects personally. The series exemplifies the British approach to literary biography and criticism at the end of the nineteenth century, and also reveals which authors were at that time regarded as canonical.

## Sir Walter Scott

Sir Walter Scott (1771–1832) is famous for his poetry and historical romances such as *Ivanhoe* and *Rob Roy*. As the first English-language author to achieve truly international fame in his lifetime, his depiction of Scottish history and culture spread around the world so effectively that it persists even today. Scott also contributed to Scottish history himself: in 1818 he helped to unearth Scotland's missing crown jewels, and he also led the campaign that saved the Scottish banknote when the London Parliament threatened its existence. First published in 1878 in the first series of 'English Men of Letters', this biography by the journalist Richard H. Hutton (1826–97) tells Scott's story from his childhood and ancestry, through his early years as an advocate to his extraordinary fame and success as a writer, through bankruptcy to recovery, and his final days.

Cambridge University Press has long been a pioneer in the reissuing of out-of-print titles from its own backlist, producing digital reprints of books that are still sought after by scholars and students but could not be reprinted economically using traditional technology. The Cambridge Library Collection extends this activity to a wider range of books which are still of importance to researchers and professionals, either for the source material they contain, or as landmarks in the history of their academic discipline.

Drawing from the world-renowned collections in the Cambridge University Library, and guided by the advice of experts in each subject area, Cambridge University Press is using state-of-the-art scanning machines in its own Printing House to capture the content of each book selected for inclusion. The files are processed to give a consistently clear, crisp image, and the books finished to the high quality standard for which the Press is recognised around the world. The latest print-on-demand technology ensures that the books will remain available indefinitely, and that orders for single or multiple copies can quickly be supplied.

The Cambridge Library Collection will bring back to life books of enduring scholarly value (including out-of-copyright works originally issued by other publishers) across a wide range of disciplines in the humanities and social sciences and in science and technology.

# Sir Walter Scott

RICHARD HOLT HUTTON

CAMBRIDGE
UNIVERSITY PRESS

CAMBRIDGE UNIVERSITY PRESS

Cambridge, New York, Melbourne, Madrid, Cape Town,
Singapore, São Paolo, Delhi, Tokyo, Mexico City

Published in the United States of America by Cambridge University Press, New York

www.cambridge.org
Information on this title: www.cambridge.org/9781108034678

© in this compilation Cambridge University Press 2011

This edition first published 1878
This digitally printed version 2011

ISBN 978-1-108-03467-8 Paperback

## English Men of Letters

### EDITED BY JOHN MORLEY

# SIR WALTER SCOTT

# SIR WALTER SCOTT

BY

RICHARD H. HUTTON

London:

MACMILLAN AND CO.

1878

LONDON:
GILBERT AND RIVINGTON, PRINTERS,
ST JOHN'S SQUARE.

# PREFATORY NOTE.

It will be observed that the greater part of this little book has been taken in one form or other from Lockhart's *Life of Sir Walter Scott*, in ten volumes. No introduction to Scott would be worth much in which that course was not followed. Indeed, excepting Sir Walter's own writings, there is hardly any other great source of information about him; and that is so full, that hardly anything needful to illustrate the subject of Scott's life remains untouched. As regards the only matters of controversy,—Scott's relations to the Ballantynes, I have taken care to check Mr. Lockhart's statements by reading those of the representatives of the Ballantyne brothers; but with this exception, Sir Walter's own works and Lockhart's life of him are the great authorities concerning his character and his story.

Just ten years ago Mr. Gladstone, in expressing to the late Mr. Hope Scott the great delight which the perusal of Lockhart's life of Sir Walter had given him, wrote, "I may be wrong, but I am vaguely under the impression that it has never had a really wide circulation. If so, it is the saddest pity, and I should greatly like (without any censure on its present length) to see published an abbreviation of it." Mr. Gladstone did not then know that as long ago as 1848 Mr. Lockhart did himself prepare such an abbreviation, in which the original eighty-four chapters were compressed into eighteen, —though the abbreviation contained additions as well as compressions. But even this abridgment is itself a bulky volume of 800 pages, containing, I should think, considerably more than a third of the reading in the original ten volumes, and is not, therefore, very likely to be preferred to the completer work. In some respects I hope that this introduction may supply, better than that bulky abbreviation, what Mr. Gladstone probably meant to suggest,—some slight miniature taken from the great picture with care enough to tempt on those who look on it to the study of the fuller life, as well as of that image of Sir Walter which is impressed by his own hand upon his works.

# CONTENTS.

# SIR WALTER SCOTT.

## CHAPTER I.

### ANCESTRY, PARENTAGE, AND CHILDHOOD.

SIR WALTER SCOTT was the first literary man of a great riding, sporting, and fighting clan. Indeed, his father—a Writer to the Signet, or Edinburgh solicitor—was the first of his race to adopt a town life and a sedentary profession. Sir Walter was the lineal descendant—six generations removed—of that Walter Scott commemorated in *The Lay of the Last Minstrel,* who is known in Border history and legend as Auld Wat of Harden. Auld Wat's son William, captured by Sir Gideon Murray, of Elibank, during a raid of the Scotts on Sir Gideon's lands, was, as tradition says, given his choice between being hanged on Sir Gideon's private gallows, and marrying the ugliest of Sir Gideon's three ugly daughters, Meikle-mouthed Meg, reputed as carrying off the prize of ugliness among the women of four counties. Sir William was a handsome man. He took three days to consider the alternative proposed to him, but chose life with the large-mouthed lady in the end; and found her, according to the tradition which the poet, her descendant, has transmitted, an excel-

lent wife, with a fine talent for pickling the beef which
her husband stole from the herds of his foes. Meikle-
mouthed Meg transmitted a distinct trace of her large
mouth to all her descendants, and not least to him
who was to use his "meikle" mouth to best advantage as the spokesman of his race. Rather more than
half-way between Auld Wat of Harden's times—i. e.,
the middle of the sixteenth century—and those of Sir
Walter Scott, poet and novelist, lived Sir Walter's
great-grandfather, Walter Scott generally known in
Teviotdale by the surname of Beardie, because he would
never cut his beard after the banishment of the Stuarts,
and who took arms in their cause and lost by his intrigues
on their behalf almost all that he had, besides running
the greatest risk of being hanged as a traitor. This was
the ancestor of whom Sir Walter speaks in the introduction to the last canto of *Marmion* :—

> " And thus my Christmas still I hold,
>   Where my great grandsire came of old,
>   With amber beard and flaxen hair,
>   And reverend apostolic air,—
>   The feast and holy tide to share,
>   And mix sobriety with wine,
>   And honest mirth with thoughts divine;
>   Small thought was his in after time
>   E'er to be hitch'd into a rhyme,
>   The simple sire could only boast
>   That he was loyal to his cost ;
>   The banish'd race of kings revered,
>   And lost his land—but kept his beard."

Sir Walter inherited from Beardie that sentimental
Stuart bias which his better judgment condemned, but
which seemed to be rather part of his blood than of his
mind. And most useful to him this sentiment un-

doubtedly was in helping him to restore the mould and
fashion of the past. Beardie's second son was Sir
Walter's grandfather, and to him he owed not only his
first childish experience of the delights of country life,
but also,—in his own estimation at least,—that risky,
speculative, and sanguine spirit which had so much influence over his fortunes. The good man of Sandy-
Knowe, wishing to breed sheep, and being destitute of
capital, borrowed 30*l.* from a shepherd who was willing
to invest that sum for him in sheep; and the two set off
to purchase a flock near Wooler, in Northumberland;
but when the shepherd had found what he thought
would suit their purpose, he returned to find his master
galloping about a fine hunter, on which he had spent
the whole capital in hand. *This* speculation, however,
prospered. A few days later Robert Scott displayed
the qualities of the hunter to such admirable effect
with John Scott of Harden's hounds, that he sold the
horse for double the money he had given, and, unlike his
grandson, abandoned speculative purchases there and
then. In the latter days of his clouded fortunes, after
Ballantyne's and Constable's failure, Sir Walter was accustomed to point to the picture of his grandfather and
say, "Blood will out: my building and planting was
but his buying the hunter before he stocked his sheep-
walk, over again." But Sir Walter added, says Mr.
Lockhart, as he glanced at the likeness of his own staid
and prudent father, " Yet it was a wonder, too, for I have
a thread of the attorney in me," which was doubtless the
case; nor was that thread the least of his inheritances,
for from his father certainly Sir Walter derived that
disposition towards conscientious, plodding industry,
legalism of mind, methodical habits of work, and a

generous, equitable interpretation of the scope of all his
obligations to others, which, prized and cultivated by
him as they were, turned a great genius, which, especially considering the hare-brained element in him, might
easily have been frittered away or devoted to worthless ends, to such fruitful account, and stamped it with
so grand an impress of personal magnanimity and fortitude.   Sir Walter's father reminds one in not a few
of the formal and rather martinetish traits which are
related of him, of the father of Goethe, "a formal man,
with strong ideas of strait-laced education, passionately
orderly (he thought a good book nothing without a good
binding), and never so much excited as by a necessary
deviation from the 'pre-established harmony' of household rules."   That description would apply almost wholly
to the sketch of old Mr. Scott which the novelist has
given us under the thin disguise of Alexander Fairford,
Writer to the Signet, in *Redgauntlet*, a figure confessedly
meant, in its chief features, to represent his father.   To
this Sir Walter adds, in one of his later journals, the
trait that his father was a man of fine presence, who conducted all conventional arrangements with a certain grandeur and dignity of air, and "absolutely loved a funeral."
" He seemed to preserve the list of a whole bead-roll of
cousins merely for the pleasure of being at their
funerals, which he was often asked to superintend, and
I suspect had sometimes to pay for.   He carried me with
him as often as he could to these mortuary ceremonies;
but feeling I was not, like him, either useful or ornamental,
I escaped as often as I could."   This strong dash of the
conventional in Scott's father, this satisfaction in seeing
people fairly to the door of life, and taking his final leave
of them there, with something of a ceremonious flourish

of observance, was, however, combined with a much
nobler and deeper kind of orderliness. Sir Walter used
to say that his father had lost no small part of a very
flourishing business, by insisting that his clients should do
their duty to their own people better than they were
themselves at all inclined to do it. And of this generous
strictness in sacrificing his own interests to his sympathy
for others, the son had as much as the father.

Sir Walter's mother, who was a Miss Rutherford, the
daughter of a physician, had been better educated than
most Scotchwomen of her day, in spite of having been
sent " to be finished off " by " the honourable Mrs.
Ogilvie," whose training was so effective, in one direction
at least, that even in her eightieth year Mrs. Scott could
not enjoy a comfortable rest in her chair, but " took as
much care to avoid touching her chair with her back, as if
she had still been under the stern eyes of Mrs. Ogilvie."
None the less Mrs. Scott was a motherly, comfortable
woman, with much tenderness of heart, and a well-stored,
vivid memory. Sir Walter, writing of her, after his
mother's death, to Lady Louisa Stewart, says, " She had
a mind peculiarly well stored with much acquired information and natural talent, and as she was very old, and
had an excellent memory, she could draw, without the
least exaggeration or affectation, the most striking pictures
of the past age. If I have been able to do anything
in the way of painting the past times, it is very much
from the studies with which she presented me. She
connected a long period of time with the present generation,
for she remembered, and had often spoken with, a person
who perfectly recollected the battle of Dunbar and Oliver
Cromwell's subsequent entry into Edinburgh." On the
day before the stroke of paralysis which carried her off, she

had told Mr. and Mrs. Scott of Harden, "with great accuracy, the real story of the Bride of Lammermuir, and pointed out wherein it differed from the novel. She had all the names of the parties, and pointed out (for she was a great genealogist) their connexion with existing families." [1] Sir Walter records many evidences of the tenderness of his mother's nature, and he returned warmly her affection for himself. His executors, in lifting up his desk, the evening after his burial, found "arranged in careful order a series of little objects, which had obviously been so placed there that his eye might rest on them every morning before he began his tasks. These were the old-fashioned boxes that had garnished his mother's toilette, when he, a sickly child, slept in her dressing-room,—the silver taper-stand, which the young advocate had bought for her with his first five-guinea fee, —a row of small packets inscribed with her hand, and containing the hair of those of her offspring that had died before her,—his father's snuff-box, and etui-case,—and more things of the like sort." [2] A story, characteristic of both Sir Walter's parents, is told by Mr. Lockhart which will serve better than anything I can remember to bring the father and mother of Scott vividly before the imagination. His father, like Mr. Alexander Fairford, in *Redgauntlet*, though himself a strong Hanoverian, inherited enough feeling for the Stuarts from his grandfather Beardie, and sympathized enough with those who were, as he neutrally expressed it, " out in '45," to ignore as much as possible any phrases offensive to the Jacobites. For instance, he always called Charles Edward not *the Pre-*

[1] Lockhart's *Life of Scott*, vi. 172-3. The edition referred to is throughout the edition of 1839 in ten volumes.

[2] Lockhart's *Life of Scott*, x. 241.

*tender* but *the Chevalier*,—and he did business for many Jacobites :—

"Mrs. Scott's curiosity was strongly excited one autumn by the regular appearance at a certain hour every evening of a sedan chair, to deposit a person carefully muffled up in a mantle, who was immediately ushered into her husband's private room, and commonly remained with him there until long after the usual bed-time of this orderly family. Mr. Scott answered her repeated inquiries with a vagueness that irritated the lady's feelings more and more; until at last she could bear the thing no longer; but one evening, just as she heard the bell ring as for the stranger's chair to carry him off, she made her appearance within the forbidden parlour with a salver in her hand, observing that she thought the gentlemen had sat so long they would be better of a dish of tea, and had ventured accordingly to bring some for their acceptance. The stranger, a person of distinguished appearance, and richly dressed, bowed to the lady and accepted a cup; but her husband knit his brows, and refused very coldly to partake the refreshment. A moment afterwards the visitor withdrew, and Mr. Scott, lifting up the window-sash, took the cup, which he had left empty on the table, and tossed it out upon the pavement. The lady exclaimed for her china, but was put to silence by her husband's saying, " I can forgive your little curiosity, madam, but you must pay the penalty. I may admit into my house, on a piece of business, persons wholly unworthy to be treated as guests by my wife. Neither lip of me nor of mine comes after Mr. Murray of Broughton's.'

"This was the unhappy man who, after attending Prince Charles Stuart as his secretary throughout the greater part of his expedition, condescended to redeem his own life and fortune by bearing evidence against the noblest of his late master's adherents, when—

"Pitied by gentle hearts, Kilmarnock died,
   The brave, Balmerino were on thy side." [1]

---

[1] Lockhart's *Life of Scott*, i. 243-4.

" Broughton's saucer "—i. e. the saucer belonging to the
cup thus sacrificed by Mr. Scott to his indignation against
one who had redeemed his own life and fortune by turning king's evidence against one of Prince Charles Stuart's
adherents,—was carefully preserved by his son, and hung
up in his first study, or "den," under a little print of
Prince Charlie.  This anecdote brings before the mind
very vividly the character of Sir Walter's parents.  The
eager curiosity of the active-minded woman, whom " the
honourable Mrs. Ogilvie " had been able to keep upright
in her chair for life, but not to cure of the desire to
unravel the little mysteries of which she had a passing
glimpse ; the grave formality of the husband, fretting
under his wife's personal attention to a dishonoured man,
and making her pay the penalty by dashing to pieces the
cup which the king's evidence had used,—again, the
visitor himself, perfectly conscious no doubt that the
Hanoverian lawyer held him in utter scorn for his faith-
lessness and cowardice, and reluctant, nevertheless, to
reject the courtesy of the wife, though he could not get
anything but cold legal advice from the husband :—all
these are figures which must have acted on the youthful
imagination of the poet with singular vivacity, and shaped
themselves in a hundred changing turns of the historical
kaleidoscope which was always before his mind's eye, as
he mused upon that past which he was to restore for us
with almost more than its original freshness of life.  With
such scenes touching even his own home, Scott must
have been constantly taught to balance in his own mind,
the more romantic, against the more sober and rational
considerations, which had so recently divided house
against house, even in the same family and clan.  That the
stern Calvinistic lawyer should have retained so much of

his grandfather Beardie's respect for the adherents of the exiled house of Stuart, must in itself have struck the boy as even more remarkable than the passionate loyalty of the Stuarts' professed partisans, and have lent a new sanction to the romantic drift of his mother's old traditions, and one to which they must have been indebted for a great part of their fascination.

Walter Scott, the ninth of twelve children, of whom the first six died in early childhood, was born in Edinburgh, on the 15th of August, 1771. Of the six later-born children, all but one were boys, and the one sister was a somewhat querulous invalid, whom he seems to have pitied almost more than he loved. At the age of eighteen months the boy had a teething-fever, ending in a life-long lameness; and this was the reason why the child was sent to reside with his grandfather—the speculative grandfather, who had doubled his capital by buying a racehorse instead of sheep—at Sandy-Knowe, near the ruined tower of Smailholm, celebrated afterwards in his ballad of *The Eve of St. John*, in the neighbourhood of some fine crags. To these crags the housemaid sent from Edinburgh to look after him, used to carry him up, with a design (which she confessed to the housekeeper)—due, of course, to incipient insanity—of murdering the child there, and burying him in the moss. Of course the maid was dismissed. After this the child used to be sent out, when the weather was fine, in the safer charge of the shepherd, who would often lay him beside the sheep. Long afterwards Scott told Mr. Skene, during an excursion with Turner, the great painter, who was drawing his illustration of Smailholm tower for one of Scott's works, that "the habit of lying on the turf there among the sheep and the lambs had given his mind a peculiar tenderness for

these animals, which it had ever since retained." Being
forgotten one day upon the knolls when a thunderstorm
came on, his aunt ran out to bring him in, and found him
shouting, "Bonny! bonny!" at every flash of lightning.
One of the old servants at Sandy-Knowe spoke of the
child long afterwards as "a sweet-tempered bairn, a
darling with all about the house," and certainly the
miniature taken of him in his seventh year confirms the
impression thus given. It is sweet-tempered above everything, and only the long upper lip and large mouth,
derived from his ancestress, Meg Murray, convey the promise of the power which was in him. Of course the high,
almost conical forehead, which gained him in his later
days from his comrades at the bar the name of "Old
Peveril," in allusion to "the peak" which they saw towering
high above the heads of other men as he approached, is not
so much marked beneath the childish locks of this miniature as it was in later life; and the massive, and, in
repose, certainly heavy face of his maturity, which conveyed the impression of the great bulk of his character, is
still quite invisible under the sunny ripple of childish
earnestness and gaiety. Scott's hair in childhood was
light chestnut, which turned to nut brown in youth. His
eyebrows were bushy, for we find mention made of them as
a "pent-house." His eyes were always light blue. They
had in them a capacity, on the one hand, for enthusiasm, sunny brightness, and even hare-brained humour,
and on the other for expressing determined resolve and
kindly irony, which gave great range of expression to
the face. There are plenty of materials for judging what
sort of a boy Scott was. In spite of his lameness, he early
taught himself to clamber about with an agility that few
children could have surpassed, and to sit his first pony—a

little Shetland, not bigger than a large Newfoundland
dog, which used to come into the house to be fed by him—
even in gallops on very rough ground.  He became very
early a declaimer.  Having learned the ballad of Hardy
Knute, he shouted it forth with such pertinacious enthusiasm that the clergyman of his grandfather's parish
complained that he "might as well speak in a cannon's
mouth as where that child was."  At six years of age Mrs.
Cockburn described him as the most astounding genius
of a boy, she ever saw.  "He was reading a poem to his
mother when I went in.  I made him read on: it was
the description of a shipwreck.  His passion rose with the
storm.  'There's the mast gone,' says he; 'crash it goes;
they will all perish.'  After his agitation he turns to me,
'That is too melancholy,' says he; 'I had better read
you something more amusing.'"  And after the call, he
told his aunt he liked Mrs. Cockburn, for "she was a
*virtuoso* like himself."  "Dear Walter," says Aunt Jenny,
"what is a *virtuoso* ?"  "Don't ye know?  Why, it's one
who wishes and will know everything."  This last scene
took place in his father's house in Edinburgh; but Scott's
life at Sandy-Knowe, including even the old minister, Dr.
Duncan, who so bitterly complained of the boy's ballad-
spouting, is painted for us, as everybody knows, in the
picture of his infancy given in the introduction to the
third canto of *Marmion* :—

> "It was a barren scene and wild,
>   Where naked cliffs were rudely piled :
>   But ever and anon between
>   Lay velvet tufts of loveliest green;
>   And well the lonely infant knew
>   Recesses where the wall-flower grew,
>   And honeysuckle loved to crawl
>   Up the low crag and ruin'd wall.

I deem'd such nooks the sweetest shade
The sun in all its round survey'd ;
And still I thought that shatter'd tower
The mightiest work of human power ;
And marvell'd as the aged hind
With some strange tale bewitch'd my mind,
Of forayers, who, with headlong force,
Down from that strength had spurr'd their horse,
Their southern rapine to renew,
Far in the distant Cheviots blue,
And, home returning, fill'd the hall
With revel, wassail-rout, and brawl.
Methought that still with trump and clang
The gateway's broken arches rang ;
Methought grim features, seam'd with scars,
Glared through the window's rusty bars ;
And ever, by the winter hearth,
Old tales I heard of woe or mirth,
Of lovers' slights, of ladies' charms,
Of witches' spells, of warriors' arms,
Of patriot battles, won of old
By Wallace wight and Bruce the bold ;
Of later fields of feud and fight,
When, pouring from their Highland height,
The Scottish clans, in headlong sway,
Had swept the scarlet ranks away.
While, stretch'd at length upon the floor,
Again I fought each combat o'er,
Pebbles and shells in order laid,
The mimic ranks of war display'd ;
And onward still the Scottish lion bore,
And still the scatter'd Southron fled before.
Still, with vain fondness, could I trace
Anew each kind familiar face
That brighten'd at our evening fire !
From the thatch'd mansion's grey-hair'd sire,
Wise without learning, plain and good,
And sprung of Scotland's gentler blood ;
Whose eye in age, quick, clear, and keen,
Show'd what in youth its glance had been ;
Whose doom discording neighbours sought,
Content with equity unbought ;

> To him the venerable priest,
> Our frequent and familiar guest,
> Whose life and manners well could paint
> Alike the student and the saint ;
> Alas ! whose speech too oft I broke
> With gambol rude and timeless joke ;
> For I was wayward, bold, and wild,
> A self-will'd imp, a grandame's child ;
> But, half a plague and half a jest,
> Was still endured, beloved, caress'd."

A picture this of a child of great spirit, though with that spirit was combined an active and subduing sweetness which could often conquer, as by a sudden spell, those whom the boy loved. Towards those, however, whom he did not love he could be vindictive. His relative, the laird of Raeburn, on one occasion wrung the neck of a pet starling, which the child had partly tamed. "I flew at his throat like a wild-cat," he said, in recalling the circumstance, fifty years later, in his journal on occasion of the old laird's death ; "and was torn from him with no little difficulty." And, judging from this journal, I doubt whether he had ever really forgiven the laird of Raeburn. Towards those whom he loved but had offended, his manner was very different. "I seldom," said one of his tutors, Mr. Mitchell, "had occasion all the time I was in the family to find fault with him, even for trifles, and only once to threaten serious castigation, of which he was no sooner aware, than he suddenly sprang up, threw his arms about my neck and kissed me." And the quaint old gentleman adds this commentary :—"By such generous and noble conduct my displeasure was in a moment converted into esteem and admiration ; my soul melted into tenderness, and I was ready to mingle my tears with his." This spontaneous and fascinating sweet-

ness of his childhood was naturally overshadowed to some
extent in later life by Scott's masculine and proud character, but it was always in him.  And there was
much of true character in the child behind this sweetness.  He had wonderful self-command, and a peremptory kind of good sense, even in his infancy.  While yet
a child under six years of age, hearing one of the servants
beginning to tell a ghost-story to another, and well knowing that if he listened, it would scare away his night's
rest, he acted for himself with all the promptness of an
elder person acting for him, and, in spite of the fascination of the subject, resolutely muffled his head in the
bed-clothes and refused to hear the tale.  His sagacity
in judging of the character of others was shown, too, even
as a school-boy ; and once it led him to take an advantage which caused him many compunctions in after-life,
whenever he recalled his skilful puerile tactics.  On one
occasion—I tell the story as he himself rehearsed it to
Samuel Rogers, almost at the end of his life, after his
attack of apoplexy, and just before leaving England
for Italy in the hopeless quest of health—he had long
desired to get above a school-fellow in his class, who
defied all his efforts, till Scott noticed that whenever a
question was asked of his rival, the lad's fingers grasped
a particular button on his waistcoat, while his mind went
in search of the answer.  Scott accordingly anticipated
that if he could remove this button, the boy would be
thrown out, and so it proved.  The button was cut off,
and the next time the lad was questioned, his fingers
being unable to find the button, and his eyes going in
perplexed search after his fingers, he stood confounded,
and Scott mastered by strategy the place which he could
not gain by mere industry.  " Often in after-life," said

Scott, in narrating the manœuvre to Rogers, "has the sight of him smote me as I passed by him; and often have I resolved to make him some reparation, but it ended in good resolutions. Though I never renewed my acquaintance with him, I often saw him, for he filled some inferior office in one of the courts of law at Edinburgh. Poor fellow! I believe he is dead; he took early to drinking."[1]

Scott's school reputation was one of irregular ability; he "glanced like a meteor from one end of the class to the other," and received more praise for his interpretation of the spirit of his authors than for his knowledge of their language. Out of school his fame stood higher. He extemporized innumerable stories to which his school-fellows delighted to listen; and, in spite of his lameness, he was always in the thick of the "bickers," or street fights with the boys of the town, and renowned for his boldness in climbing the "kittle nine stanes" which are "projected high in air from the precipitous black granite of the Castle-rock." At home he was much bullied by his elder brother Robert, a lively lad, not without some powers of verse-making, who went into the navy, then in an unlucky moment passed into the merchant service of the East India Company, and so lost the chance of distinguishing himself in the great naval campaigns of Nelson. Perhaps Scott would have been all the better for a sister a little closer to him than Anne—sickly and fanciful—appears ever to have been. The masculine side of life appears to predominate a little too much in his school and college days, and he had such vast energy, vitality, and pride, that his life at this time would have borne a little taming under the influence of a sister thoroughly

---

[1] Lockhart's *Life of Scott*, i. 128.

congenial to him. In relation to his studies he was
wilful, though not perhaps perverse. He steadily declined, for instance, to learn Greek, though he mastered
Latin pretty fairly. After a time spent at the High
School, Edinburgh, Scott was sent to a school at Kelso,
where his master made a friend and companion of him,
and so poured into him a certain amount of Latin scholar-
ship which he would never otherwise have obtained. I
need hardly add that as a boy Scott was, so far as a boy
could be, a Tory—a worshipper of the past, and a great
Conservative of any remnant of the past which reformers
wished to get rid of. In the autobiographical fragment
of 1808, he says, in relation to these school-days, " I,
with my head on fire for chivalry, was a Cavalier ; my
friend was a Roundhead ; I was a Tory, and he was a
Whig ; I hated Presbyterians, and admired Montrose
with his victorious Highlanders ; he liked the Presby-
terian Ulysses, the deep and politic Argyle ; so that we
never wanted subjects of dispute, but our disputes were
always amicable." And he adds candidly enough : " In
all these tenets there was no real conviction on my part,
arising out of acquaintance with the views or principles
of either party. . . . . I took up politics at that
period, as King Charles II. did his religion, from an idea
that the Cavalier creed was the more gentlemanlike per-
suasion of the two." And the uniformly amicable character
of these controversies between the young people, itself
shows how much more they were controversies of the
imagination than of faith. I doubt whether Scott's *con-
victions* on the issues of the Past were ever very much
more decided than they were during his boyhood ; though
undoubtedly he learned to understand much more pro-
foundly what was really held by the ablest men on both

sides of these disputed issues.   The result, however, was,
I think, that while he entered  better and better into both
sides  as  life went on, he never  adopted  either with any
earnestness  of  conviction,  being  content  to  admit,  even
to himself, that while his feelings  leaned in one direction,
his  reason  pointed  decidedly in  the  other ;  and  holding
that it  was  hardly needful to  identify himself  positively
with  either.   As  regarded  the  present, however, feeling
always carried the day.   Scott was a Tory all his life.

## CHAPTER II.

### YOUTH—CHOICE OF A PROFESSION.

As Scott grew up, entered the classes of the college, and
began his legal studies, first as apprentice to his father,
and then in the law classes of the University, he became
noticeable to all his friends for his gigantic memory,—the
rich stores of romantic material with which it was loaded,
—his giant feats of industry for any cherished purpose,—
his delight in adventure and in all athletic enterprises,—
his great enjoyment of youthful " rows," so long as they
did not divide the knot of friends to which he belonged,
and his skill in peacemaking amongst his own set.  During
his apprenticeship his only means of increasing his slender
allowance with funds which he could devote to his
favourite studies, was to earn money by copying, and he
tells us himself that he remembered writing " 120 folio
pages with no interval either for food or rest," fourteen
or fifteen hours' very hard work at the very least,—
expressly for this purpose.

In the second year of Scott's apprenticeship, at about
the age of sixteen, he had an attack of hæmorrhage,
no recurrence of which took place for some forty
years, but which was then the beginning of the end.
During this illness silence was absolutely imposed
upon him,—two old ladies putting their fingers on

their lips whenever he offered to speak. It was at this
time that the lad began his study of the scenic side of
history, and especially of campaigns, which he illustrated
for himself by the arrangement of shells, seeds, and
pebbles, so as to represent encountering armies, in the
manner referred to (and referred to apparently in anticipation of a later stage of his life than that he was then speaking of) in the passage from the introduction to the third
canto of *Marmion* which I have already given. He also
managed so to arrange the looking-glasses in his room as
to see the troops march out to exercise in the meadows,
as he lay in bed. His reading was almost all in the
direction of military exploit, or romance and mediæval legend and the later border songs of his own
country. He learned Italian and read Ariosto. Later
he learned Spanish and devoured Cervantes, whose
"*novelas*," he said, "first inspired him with the ambition
to excel in fiction;" and all that he read and admired
he remembered. Scott used to illustrate the capricious
affinity of his own memory for what suited it, and its
complete rejection of what did not, by old Beattie of
Meikledale's answer to a Scotch divine, who complimented
him on the strength of his memory. "No, sir," said the
old Borderer, "I have no command of my memory. It
only retains what hits my fancy; and probably, sir,
if you were to preach to me for two hours, I would not
be able, when you finished, to remember a word you had
been saying." Such a memory, when it belongs to a man
of genius, is really a sieve of the most valuable kind.
It sifts away what is foreign and alien to his genius, and
assimilates what is suited to it. In his very last days,
when he was visiting Italy for the first time, Scott delighted
in Malta, for it recalled to him Vertot's *Knights of Malta*,

and much other mediæval story which he had pored over
in his youth. But when his friends descanted to him at
Pozzuoli on the Thermæ—commonly called the Temple
of Serapis—among the ruins of which he stood, he only
remarked that he would believe whatever he was told,
"for many of his friends, and particularly Mr. Morritt,
had frequently tried to drive classical antiquities, as they
are called, into his head, but they had always found his
skull too thick." Was it not perhaps some deep literary
instinct, like that here indicated, which made him, as a
lad, refuse so steadily to learn Greek, and try to prove to
his indignant professor that Ariosto was superior to
Homer? Scott afterwards deeply regretted this neglect
of Greek ; but I cannot help thinking that his regret was
misplaced. Greek literature would have brought before
his mind standards of poetry and art which could not
but have both deeply impressed and greatly daunted an
intellect of so much power ; I say both impressed and
daunted, because I believe that Scott himself would never
have succeeded in studies of a classical kind, while he
might—like Goethe perhaps—have been either misled, by
admiration for that school, into attempting what was not
adapted to his genius, or else disheartened in the work
for which his character and ancestry really fitted him.
It has been said that there is a real affinity between Scott
and Homer. But the long and refluent music of Homer,
once naturalized in his mind, would have discontented
him with that quick, sharp, metrical tramp of his own moss-
troopers, to which alone his genius as a poet was perfectly suited.

It might be supposed that with these romantic tastes,
Scott could scarcely have made much of a lawyer, though
the inference would, I believe, be quite mistaken. His

father, however, reproached him with being better fitted for
a pedlar than a lawyer,—so persistently did he trudge over
all the neighbouring counties in search of the beauties
of nature and the historic associations of battle, siege, or
legend.  On one occasion when, with their last penny spent,
Scott and one of his companions had returned to Edinburgh, living during their last day on drinks of milk
offered by generous peasant-women, and the hips and haws
on the hedges, he remarked to his father how much he
had wished for George Primrose's power of playing on the
flute in order to earn a meal by the way, old Mr. Scott,
catching grumpily at the idea, replied, "I greatly doubt, sir,
you were born for nae better then a gangrel scrape-gut,"—
a speech which very probably suggested his son's conception of Darsie Latimer's adventures with the blind fiddler,
"Wandering Willie," in *Redgauntlet*.  And, it is true that
these were the days of mental and moral fermentation,
what was called in Germany the Sturm-und-Drang, the
"fret-and-fury" period of Scott's life, so far as one so
mellow and genial in temper ever passed through a period
of fret and fury at all.  In other words these were the days
of rapid motion, of walks of thirty miles a day which
the lame lad yet found no fatigue to him; of mad enterprises, scrapes and drinking-bouts, in one of which Scott
was half persuaded by his friends that he actually sang
a song for the only time in his life.  But even in these
days of youthful sociability, with companions of his
own age, Scott was always himself, and his imperious will
often asserted itself.  Writing of this time, some thirty-
five years or so later, he said, "When I was a boy, and
on foot expeditions, as we had many, no creature could be
so indifferent which way our course was directed, and I
acquiesced in what any one proposed; but if I was once

driven to make a choice, and felt piqued in honour to maintain my proposition, I have broken off from the whole party, rather than yield to any one." No doubt, too, in that day of what he himself described as "the silly smart fancies that ran in my brain like the bubbles in a glass of champagne, as brilliant to my thinking, as intoxicating, as evanescent," solitude was no real deprivation to him; and one can easily imagine him marching off on his solitary way after a dispute with his companions, reciting to himself old songs or ballads, with that "noticeable but altogether indescribable play of the upper lip," which Mr. Lockhart thinks suggested to one of Scott's most intimate friends, on his first acquaintance with him, the grotesque notion that he had been "a hautboy-player." This was the first impression formed of Scott by William Clerk, one of his earliest and lifelong friends. It greatly amused Scott, who not only had never played on any instrument in his life, but could hardly make shift to join in the chorus of a popular song without marring its effect; but perhaps the impression suggested was not so very far astray after all. Looking to the poetic side of his character, the trumpet certainly would have been the instrument that would have best symbolized the spirit both of Scott's thought and of his verses. Mr. Lockhart himself, in summing up his impressions of Sir Walter, quotes as the most expressive of his lines :—

> " Sound, sound the clarion ! fill the fife !
>     To all the sensual world proclaim,
>     One crowded hour of glorious life
>     Is worth a world without a name."

And undoubtedly this gives us the key-note of Scott's personal life as well as of his poetic power. Above every-

thing he was high-spirited, a man of noble, and, at the same
time, of martial feelings.   Sir Francis Doyle speaks very
justly of Sir Walter as "among English singers the
undoubted inheritor of that trumpet-note, which, under
the breath of Homer, has made the wrath of Achilles
immortal;" and I do not doubt that there was something
in Scott's face, and especially in the expression of his
mouth, to suggest this even to his early college companions.   Unfortunately, however, even "one crowded
hour of glorious life" may sometimes have a "sensual"
inspiration, and in these days of youthful adventure, too
many such hours seem to have owed their inspiration
to the Scottish peasant's chief bane, the Highland whisky.
In his eager search after the old ballads of the Border,
Scott had many a blithe adventure, which ended only too
often in a carouse.   It was soon after this time that he first
began those raids into Liddesdale, of which all the world
has enjoyed the records in the sketches—embodied subsequently in *Guy Mannering*—of Dandie Dinmont, his pony
Dumple, and the various Peppers and Mustards from
whose breed there were afterwards introduced into Scott's
own family, generations of terriers, always named, as Sir
Walter expressed it, after "the cruet."   I must quote the
now classic record of those youthful escapades :—

"Eh me," said Mr. Shortreed, his companion in all these
Liddesdale raids, "sic an endless fund of humour and drollery
as he had then wi' him.   Never ten yards but we were either
laughing or roaring and singing.   Wherever we stopped, how
brawlie he suited himsel' to everybody !   He aye did as the
lave did ; never made himsel' the great man or took ony airs
in the company.   I've seen him in a' moods in these jaunts,
grave and gay, daft and serious, sober and drunk—(this, however, even in our wildest rambles, was but rare)—but drunk
or sober he was aye the gentleman.   He looked excessively

heavy and stupid when he was *fou,* but he was never out o'
gude humour."

One of the stories of that time will illustrate better
the wilder days of Scott's youth than any comment :—

"On reaching one evening," says Mr. Lockhart, some
Charlieshope or other (I forget the name) among those wil-
dernesses, they found a kindly reception as usual : but to
their agreeable surprise, after some days of hard living, a
measured and orderly hospitality as respected liquor.   Soon
after supper, at which a bottle of elderberry wine alone had
been produced, a young student of divinity who happened to
be in the house was called upon to take the ' big ha' Bible,' in
the good old fashion of Burns' Saturday Night : and some
progress had been already made in the service, when the good
man of the farm, whose 'tendency,' as Mr. Mitchell says,
' was soporific,' scandalized his wife and the dominie by start-
ing suddenly from his knees, and rubbing his eyes, with a
stentorian exclamation of ' By —— ! here's the keg at last ! '
and in tumbled, as he spake the word, a couple of sturdy
herdsmen, whom, on hearing, a day before, of the advocate's
approaching visit, he had despatched to a certain smuggler's
haunt at some considerable distance in quest of a supply of
*run* brandy from the Solway frith.   The pious 'exercise' of
the household was hopelessly interrupted.   With a thousand
apologies for his hitherto shabby entertainment, this jolly
Elliot or Armstrong had the welcome *keg* mounted on the
table without a moment's delay, and gentle and simple, not
forgetting the dominie, continued carousing about it until
daylight streamed in upon the party.   Sir Walter Scott
seldom failed, when I saw him in company with his Liddesdale companions, to mimic with infinite humour the sudden
outburst of his old host on hearing the clatter of horses' feet,
which he knew to indicate the arrival of the keg, the con-
sternation of the dame, and the rueful despair with which
the young clergyman closed the book."[1]

---

[1] Lockhart's *Life of Scott,* i. 269-71.

No wonder old Mr. Scott felt some doubt of his son's success at the bar, and thought him more fitted in many respects for a " gangrel scrape-gut."[1]

In spite of all this love of excitement, Scott became a sound lawyer, and might have been a great lawyer, had not his pride of character, the impatience of his genius, and the stir of his imagination rendered him indisposed to wait and slave in the precise manner which the prepossessions of solicitors appoint.

For Scott's passion for romantic literature was not at all the sort of thing which we ordinarily mean by boys' or girls' love of romance. No amount of drudgery or labour deterred Scott from any undertaking on the prosecution of which he was bent. He was quite the reverse, indeed, of what is usually meant by sentimental, either in his manners or his literary interests. As regards the history of his own country he was no mean antiquarian. Indeed he cared for the mustiest antiquarian researches— of the mediæval kind—so much, that in the depth of his troubles he speaks of a talk with a Scotch antiquary and herald as one of the things which soothed him most. " I do not know anything which relieves the mind so much from the sullens as trifling discussions about anti-quarian *old womanries*. It is like knitting a stocking, diverting the mind without occupying it." [2]    Thus his love of romantic literature was as far as possible from that of a mind which only feeds on romantic excitements ; rather was it that of one who was so moulded by the transmitted and acquired love of feudal institutions with all their incidents, that he could not take any deep interest in any other

---

[1] Lockhart's *Life of Scott*, i. 206.
[2] Lockhart's *Life of Scott*, ix. 221.

fashion of human society. Now the Scotch law was full
of vestiges and records of that period,—was indeed a great
standing monument of it ; and in numbers of his writings
Scott shows with how deep an interest he had studied
the Scotch law from this point of view. He remarks somewhere that it was natural for a Scotchman to feel a strong
attachment to the principle of rank, if only on the ground
that almost any Scotchman might, under the Scotch law,
turn out to be heir-in-tail to some great Scotch title or
estate by the death of intervening relations. And the law
which sometimes caused such sudden transformations, had
subsequently a true interest for him of course as a novel
writer, to say nothing of his interest in it as an antiquarian and historian who loved to repeople the earth, not
merely with the picturesque groups of the soldiers and
courts of the past, but with the actors in all the various
quaint and homely transactions and puzzlements which
the feudal ages had brought forth. Hence though, as a
matter of fact, Scott never made much figure as an advocate, he became a very respectable, and might unquestionably have become a very great, lawyer. When he started
at the bar, however, he had not acquired the tact to
impress an ordinary assembly. In one case which he
conducted before the General Assembly of the Kirk of
Scotland, when defending a parish minister threatened
with deposition for drunkenness and unseemly behaviour,
he certainly missed the proper tone,—first receiving a
censure for the freedom of his manner in treating the alle-
gations against his client, and then so far collapsing under
the rebuke of the Moderator, as to lose the force and ur-
gency necessary to produce an effect on his audience. But
these were merely a boy's mishaps. He was certainly by
no means a Heaven-born orator, and therefore could not

expect to spring into exceptionally *early* distinction, and the only true reason for his relative failure was that he was so full of literary power, and so proudly impatient of the fetters which prudence seemed to impose on his extra-professional proceedings, that he never gained the credit he deserved for the general common sense, the unwearied industry, and the keen appreciation of the ins and outs of legal method, which might have raised him to the highest reputation even as a judge.

All readers of his novels know how Scott delights in the humours of the law.  By way of illustration take the following passage, which is both short and amusing, in which Saunders Fairford—the old solicitor painted from Scott's father in *Redgauntlet*—descants on the law of the stirrup-cup.  " It was decided in a case before the town bailies of Cupar Angus, when Luckie Simpson's cow had drunk up Luckie Jamieson's browst of ale, while it stood in the door to cool, that there was no damage to pay, because the crummie drank without sitting down ; such being the circumstance constituting a Doch an Dorroch, which is a standing drink for which no reckoning is paid."  I do not believe that any one of Scott's contemporaries had greater legal abilities than he, though, as it happened, they were never fairly tried.  But he had both the pride and impatience of genius.  It fretted him to feel that he was dependent on the good opinions of solicitors, and that they who were incapable of understanding his genius, thought the less instead of the better of him as an advocate, for every indication which he gave of that genius.  Even on the day of his call to the bar he gave expression to a sort of humorous foretaste of this impatience, saying to William Clerk, who had been called with him, as he mimicked the air and tone of a Highland

lass waiting at the Cross of Edinburgh to be hired for the
harvest, " We've stood here an hour by the Tron, hinny,
and deil a ane has speered our price." Scott continued to
practise at the bar—nominally at least — for fourteen
years, but the most which he ever seems to have made in
any one year was short of 230*l.*, and latterly his practice
was much diminishing instead of increasing. His own
impatience of solicitors' patronage was against him ; his
well-known dabblings in poetry were still more against
him ; and his general repute for wild and unprofessional ad-
venturousness—which was much greater than he deserved
—was probably most of all against him. Before he had
been six years at the bar he joined the organization of the
Edinburgh Volunteer Cavalry, took a very active part in
the drill, and was made their Quartermaster. Then he
visited London, and became largely known for his
ballads, and his love of ballads. In his eighth year
at the bar he accepted a small permanent appointment,
with 300*l.* a year, as sheriff of Selkirkshire ; and this
occurring soon after his marriage to a lady of some
means, no doubt diminished still further his professional zeal. For one third of the time during which
Scott practised as an advocate he made no pretence of
taking interest in that part of his work, though he was
always deeply interested in the law itself. In 1806 he
undertook gratuitously the duties of a Clerk of Session—
a permanent officer of the Court at Edinburgh—and discharged them without remuneration for five years, from
1806 to 1811, in order to secure his ultimate succession to
the office in the place of an invalid, who for that
period received all the emoluments and did none of the
work. Nevertheless Scott's legal abilities were so well
known, that it was certainly at one time intended to offer

him a Barony of the Exchequer, and it was his own doing, apparently, that it was not offered.    The life of literature and the life of the Bar hardly ever suit, and in Scott's case they suited the less, that he felt himself likely to be a dictator in the one field, and only a postulant in the other.    Literature was a far greater gainer by his choice, than Law could have been a loser.    For his capacity for the law he shared with thousands of able men, his capacity for literature with few or none.

## CHAPTER III

### LOVE AND MARRIAGE.

ONE Sunday, about two years before his call to the bar,
Scott offered his umbrella to a young lady of much
beauty who was coming out of the Greyfriars Church
during a shower; the umbrella was graciously accepted;
and it was not an unprecedented consequence that Scott
fell in love with the borrower, who turned out to be
Margaret, daughter of Sir John and Lady Jane Stuart
Belches, of Invernay. For near six years after this,
Scott indulged the hope of marrying this lady, and it
does not seem doubtful that the lady herself was in
part responsible for this impression. Scott's father, who
thought his son's prospects very inferior to those of Miss
Stuart Belches, felt it his duty to warn the baronet of
his son's views, a warning which the old gentleman
appears to have received with that grand unconcern
characteristic of elderly persons in high position, as a
hint intrinsically incredible, or at least unworthy of
notice. But he took no alarm, and Scott's attentions to
Margaret Stuart Belches continued till close on the eve
of her marriage, in 1796, to William Forbes (afterwards
Sir William Forbes), of Pitsligo, a banker, who proved
to be one of Sir Walter's most generous and most
delicate-minded friends, when his time of troubles came

towards the end of both their lives. Whether Scott was
in part mistaken as to the impression he had made on
the young lady, or she was mistaken as to the impression
he had made on herself, or whether other circumstances
intervened to cause misunderstanding, or the grand indifference of Sir John gave way to active intervention
when the question became a practical one, the world will
now never know, but it does not seem very likely that
a man of so much force as Scott, who certainly had at
one time assured himself at least of the young lady's
strong regard, should have been easily displaced even by
a rival of ability and of most generous and amiable
character. An entry in the diary which Scott kept in
1827, after Constable's and Ballantyne's failure, and his
wife's death, seems to me to suggest that there may have
been some misunderstanding between the young people,
though I am not sure that the inference is justified.
The passage completes the story of this passion—Scott's
first and only deep passion—so far as it can ever be
known to us; and as it is a very pathetic and characteristic entry, and the attachment to which it refers had
a great influence on Scott's life, both in keeping him free
from some of the most dangerous temptations of the
young, during his youth, and in creating within him
an interior world of dreams and recollections throughout
his whole life, on which his imaginative nature was con-
tinually fed—I may as well give it. " He had taken,"
says Mr. Lockhart, "for that winter [1827], the house
No. 6, Shandwick Place, which he occupied by the
month during the remainder of his servitude as a clerk
of session. Very near this house, he was told a few
days after he took possession, dwelt the aged mother of
his first love ; and he expressed to his friend Mrs.

Skene, a wish that she should carry him to renew an
acquaintance which seems to have been interrupted from
the period of his youthful romance. Mrs. Skene com-
plied with his desire, and she tells me that a very
painful scene ensued." His diary says,—" November
7th. Began to settle myself this morning after the hurry
of mind and even of body which I have lately under-
gone. I went to make a visit and fairly softened
myself, like an old fool, with recalling old stories till
I was fit for nothing but shedding tears and repeating
verses for the whole night. This is sad work. The very
grave gives up its dead, and time rolls back thirty years
to add to my perplexities. I don't care. I begin to
grow case-hardened, and like a stag turning at bay,
my naturally good temper grows fierce and dangerous.
Yet what a romance to tell—and told I fear it will one
day be. And then my three years of dreaming and my
two years of wakening will be chronicled, doubtless. But
the dead will feel no pain.—November 10th. At twelve
o'clock I went again to poor Lady Jane to talk over old
stories. I am not clear that it is a right or healthful
indulgence to be ripping up old sores, but it seems to
give her deep-rooted sorrow words, and that is a mental
blood-letting. To me these things are now matter of calm
and solemn recollection, never to be forgotten, yet scarce
to be remembered with pain." [1] It was in 1797, after
the break-up of his hopes in relation to this attachment,
that Scott wrote the lines *To a Violet*, which Mr. F. T. Pal-
grave, in his thoughtful and striking introduction to Scott's
poems, rightly characterize sas one of the most beautiful
of those poems. It is, however, far from one character-

[1] Lockhart's *Life of Scott*, ix. 183-4.

istic of Scott, indeed, so different in style from the best
of his other poems, that Mr. Browning might well have
said of Scott, as he once affirmed of himself, that for
the purpose of one particular poem, he "who blows
through bronze," had "breathed through silver,"—had
"curbed the liberal hand `subservient proudly,"—and
tamed his spirit to a key elsewhere unknown.

> "The violet in her greenwood bower,
>     Where birchen boughs with hazels mingle,
> May boast itself the fairest flower
>     In glen, or copse, or forest dingle.
>
> "Though fair her gems of azure hue,
>     Beneath the dewdrop's weight reclining,
> I've seen an eye of lovelier blue,
>     More sweet through watery lustre shining.
>
> "The summer sun that dew shall dry,
>     Ere yet the day be past its morrow;
> Nor longer in my false love's eye
>     Remain'd the tear of parting sorrow."

These lines obviously betray a feeling of resentment,
which may or may not have been justified; but they are
perhaps the most delicate produced by his pen.  The
pride which was always so notable a feature in Scott, probably sustained him through the keen, inward pain which
it is very certain from a great many of his own words that
he must have suffered in this uprooting of his most passionate hopes.  And it was in part probably the same
pride which led him to form, within the year, a new tie—
his engagement to Mademoiselle Charpentier, or Miss
Carpenter as she was usually called,—the daughter of a
French royalist of Lyons who had died early in the revolution.  She had come after her father's death to England, chiefly, it seems, because in the Marquis of Down-

shire, who was an old friend of the family, her mother knew
that she should find a protector for her children.   Miss
Carpenter was a lively beauty, probably of no great depth
of character.   The few letters given of hers in Mr. Lockhart's life of Scott, give the impression of an amiable,
petted girl, of somewhat thin and *espiègle* character,
who was rather charmed at the depth and intensity of
Scott's nature, and at the expectations which he seemed
to form of what love should mean, than capable of realizing them.   Evidently she had no inconsiderable pleasure in
display; but she made on the whole a very good wife, only
one to be protected by him from every care, and not one
to share Scott's deeper anxieties, or to participate in his
dreams.   Yet Mrs. Scott was not devoid of spirit and self-
control.   For instance, when Mr. Jeffrey, having reviewed
*Marmion* in the *Edinburgh* in that depreciating and om-
niscient tone which was then considered the evidence of
critical acumen, dined with Scott on the very day on
which the review had appeared, Mrs. Scott behaved to
him through the whole evening with the greatest politeness, but fired this parting shot in her broken English,
as he took his leave,—" Well, good night, Mr. Jeffrey,—
dey tell me you have abused Scott in de *Review*, and I
hope Mr. Constable has paid you very well for writing
it."   It is hinted that Mrs. Scott was, at the time of
Scott's greatest fame, far more exhilarated by it than her
husband with his strong sense and sure self-measurement
ever was.   Mr. Lockhart records that Mrs. Grant of Laggan
once said of them, " Mr. Scott always seems to me like a
glass, through which the rays of admiration pass without
sensibly affecting it; but the bit of paper that lies beside
it will presently be in a blaze, and no wonder."   The bit
of paper, however, never was in a blaze that I know of;

and possibly Mrs. Grant's remark may have had a little
feminine spite in it.　At all events, it was not till the rays
of misfortune, instead of admiration, fell upon Scott's life,
that the delicate tissue paper shrivelled up; nor does it
seem that, even then, it was the trouble, so much as a
serious malady that had fixed on Lady Scott before Sir
Walter's troubles began, which really scorched up her
life.　That she did not feel with the depth and intensity
of her husband, or in the same key of feeling, is clear.
After the failure, and during the preparations for abandon-
ing the house in Edinburgh, Scott records in his diary :—
" It is with a sense of pain that I leave behind a parcel
of trumpery prints and little ornaments, once the pride
of Lady Scott's heart, but which she saw consigned with
indifference to the chance of an auction.　Things that have
had their day of importance with me, I cannot forget,
though the merest trifles; but I am glad that she, with
bad health, and enough to vex her, has not the same useless mode of associating recollections with this unpleasant
business." [1]

Poor Lady Scott !　It was rather like a bird of paradise
mating with an eagle.　Yet the result was happy on the
whole; for she had a thoroughly kindly nature, and a true
heart.　Within ten days before her death, Scott enters in
his diary :—" Still welcoming me with a smile, and assert-
ing she is better."　She was not the ideal wife for Scott;
but she loved him, sunned herself in his prosperity, and
tried to bear his adversity cheerfully.　In her last illness
she would always reproach her husband and children for
their melancholy faces, even when that melancholy was, as
she well knew, due to the approaching shadow of her own
death.

[1] Lockhart's *Life of Scott*, viii. 273.

D 2

## CHAPTER IV.

### EARLIEST POETRY AND BORDER MINSTRELSY.

SCOTT's first serious attempt in poetry was a version of Bürger's *Lenore,* a spectre-ballad of the violent kind, much in favour in Germany at a somewhat earlier period, but certainly not a specimen of the higher order of imaginative genius. However, it stirred Scott's youthful blood, and made him "wish to heaven he could get a skull and two cross-bones!" a modest desire, to be expressed with so much fervour, and one almost immediately gratified. Probably no one ever gave a more spirited version of Bürger's ballad than Scott has given ; but the use to which Miss Cranstoun, a friend and confidante of his love for Miss Stuart Belches, strove to turn it, by getting it printed, blazoned, and richly bound, and presenting it to the young lady as a proof of her admirer's abilities, was perhaps hardly very sagacious. It is quite possible, at least, that Miss Stuart Belches may have regarded this vehement admirer of spectral wedding journeys and skeleton bridals, as unlikely to prepare for her that comfortable, trim, and decorous future which young ladies usually desire. At any rate, the bold stroke failed. The young lady admired the verses, but, as we have seen, declined the translator. Perhaps she regarded banking as safer, if less brilliant, work than the most

effective description of skeleton riders.   Indeed, Scott at
this time—to those who did not know what was in him,
which no one, not even excepting himself, did—had no
very sure prospects of comfort, to say nothing of wealth.
It is curious, too, that his first adventure in literature was
thus connected with his interest in the preternatural, for
no man ever lived whose genius was sounder and healthier,
and less disposed to dwell on the half-and-half lights of a
dim and eerie world ; yet ghostly subjects always interested
him deeply, and he often touched them in his stories, more,
I think, from the strong artistic contrast they afforded to
his favourite conceptions of life, than from any other
motive.   There never was, I fancy, an organization less
susceptible of this order of fears and superstitions than his
own.   When a friend jokingly urged him, within a few
months of his death, not to leave Rome on a Friday, as it
was a day of bad omen for a journey, he replied, laughing,
" Superstition is very picturesque, and I make it, at times,
stand me in great stead, but I never allow it to interfere
with interest or convenience."   Basil Hall reports Scott's
having told him on the last evening of the year 1824,
when they were talking over this subject, that "having
once arrived at a country inn, he was told there was no
bed for him. 'No place to lie down at all?' said he.
'No,' said the people of the house ; 'none, except a room
in which there is a corpse lying.' 'Well,' said he, 'did
the person die of any contagious disorder?' 'Oh, no ;
not at all,' said they. 'Well, then,' continued he, 'let
me have the other bed. So,' said Sir Walter, 'I laid me
down, and never had a better night's sleep in my life.'"
He was, indeed, a man of iron nerve, whose truest artistic
enjoyment was in noting the forms of character seen in
full daylight by the light of the most ordinary experience.

Perhaps for that reason he can on occasion relate a
preternatural incident, such as the appearance of old Alice
at the fountain, at the very moment of her death, to the
Master of Ravenswood, in *The Bride of Lammermoor*,
with great effect. It was probably the vivacity with
which he realized the violence which such incidents do to
the terrestrial common sense of our ordinary nature, and
at the same time the sedulous accuracy of detail with
which he narrated them, rather than any, even the
smallest, special susceptibility of his own brain to thrills
of the preternatural kind, which gave him rather a unique
pleasure in dealing with such preternatural elements.
Sometimes, however, his ghosts are a little too muscular
to produce their due effect as ghosts. In translating
Bürger's ballad his great success lay in the vividness of the
spectre's horsemanship. For instance,—

> "Tramp! tramp! along the land they rode,
>   Splash! splash! along the sea;
> The scourge is red, the spur drops blood,
>   The flashing pebbles flee,"

is far better than any ghostly touch in it; so, too, every
one will remember how spirited a rider is the white Lady
of Avenel, in *The Monastery*, and how vigorously she
takes fords,—as vigorously as the sheriff himself, who was
very fond of fords. On the whole, Scott was too sunny
and healthy-minded for a ghost-seer; and the skull and
cross-bones with which he ornamented his " den " in his
father's house, did not succeed in tempting him into the
world of twilight and cobwebs wherein he made his first
literary excursion. His *William and Helen*, the name he
gave to his translation of Bürger's *Lenore*, made in 1795,
was effective, after all, more for its rapid movement, than
for the weirdness of its effects.

If, however, it was the raw preternaturalism of such ballads as Bürger's which first led Scott to test his own powers, his genius soon turned to more appropriate and natural subjects. Ever since his earliest college days he had been collecting, in those excursions of his into Liddesdale and elsewhere, materials for a book on *The Minstrelsy of the Scottish Border ;* and the publication of this work, in January, 1802 (in two volumes at first), was his first great literary success. The whole edition of eight hundred copies was sold within the year, while the skill and care which Scott had devoted to the historical illustration of the ballads, and the force and spirit of his own new ballads, written in imitation of the old, gained him at once a very high literary name. And the name was well deserved. The *Border Minstrelsy* was more commensurate *in range* with the genius of Scott, than even the romantic poems by which it was soon followed, and which were received with such universal and almost unparalleled delight. For Scott's *Border Minstrelsy* gives more than a glimpse of all his many great powers—his historical industry and knowledge, his masculine humour, his delight in restoring the vision of the " old, simple, violent world " of rugged activity and excitement, as well as that power to kindle men's hearts, as by a trumpet-call, which was the chief secret of the charm of his own greatest poems. It is much easier to discern the great novelist of subsequent years in the *Border Minstrelsy* than even in *The Lay of the Last Minstrel, Marmion,* and *The Lady of the Lake* taken together. From those romantic poems you would never guess that Scott entered more eagerly and heartily into the common incidents and common cares of every-day human life than into the most romantic fortunes ; from them you would never know how com-

pletely he had mastered the leading features of quite
different periods of our history ; from them you would
never infer that you had before you one of the best
plodders, as well as one of the most enthusiastic dreamers,
in British literature. But all this might have been
gathered from the various introductions and notes to the
*Border Minstrelsy*, which are full of skilful illustrations,
of comments teeming with humour, and of historic weight.
The general introduction gives us a general survey of the
graphic pictures of Border quarrels, their simple violence
and simple cunning. It enters, for instance, with grave
humour into the strong distinction taken in the debatable
land between a "freebooter" and a "thief," and the difficulty which the inland counties had in grasping it, and
paints for us, with great vivacity, the various Border superstitions. Another commentary on a very amusing ballad,
commemorating the manner in which a blind harper stole
a horse and got paid for a mare he had not lost, gives
an account of the curious tenure of land, called that of
the "king's rentallers," or "kindly tenants;" and a third
describes, in language as vivid as the historical romance
of *Kenilworth*, written years after, the manner in which
Queen Elizabeth received the news of a check to her
policy, and vented her spleen on the King of Scotland.

So much as to the breadth of the literary area which
this first book of Scott's covered. As regards the poetic
power which his own new ballads, in imitation of the
old ones, evinced, I cannot say that those of the first
issue of the *Border Minstrelsy* indicated anything like the
force which might have been expected from one who was
so soon to be the author of *Marmion*, though many of
Scott's warmest admirers, including Sir Francis Doyle,
seem to place *Glenfinlas* among his finest productions. But

in the third volume of the *Border Minstrelsy*, which did
not appear till 1803, is contained a ballad on the assas-
sination of the Regent Murray, the story being told
by his assassin, which seems to me a specimen of his very
highest poetical powers. In *Cadyow Castle* you have not
only that rousing trumpet-note which you hear in *Marmion*, but the pomp and glitter of a grand martial scene is
painted with all Scott's peculiar terseness and vigour.
The opening is singularly happy in preparing the reader
for the description of a violent deed. The Earl of Arran,
chief of the clan of Hamiltons, is chasing among the old
oaks of Cadyow Castle,—oaks which belonged to the
ancient Caledonian forest,—the fierce, wild bulls, milk-
white, with black muzzles, which were not extirpated till
shortly before Scott's own birth :—

> " Through the huge oaks of Evandale,
>     Whose limbs a thousand years have worn,
> What sullen roar comes down the gale,
>     And drowns the hunter's pealing horn ?
>
> " Mightiest of all the beasts of chase
>     That roam in woody Caledon,
> Crashing the forest in his race,
>     The mountain bull comes thundering on.
>
> " Fierce on the hunter's quiver'd band
>     He rolls his eyes of swarthy glow,
> Spurns, with black hoof and horn, the sand,
>     And tosses high his mane of snow.
>
> " Aim'd well, the chieftain's lance has flown ;
>     Struggling in blood the savage lies ;
> His roar is sunk in hollow groan,—
>     Sound, merry huntsman ! sound the pryse ! "

It is while the hunters are resting after this feat, that
Bothwellhaugh dashes among them headlong, spurring
his jaded steed with poniard instead of spur :—

> " From gory selle and reeling steed,
>     Sprang the fierce horseman with a bound,
> And reeking from the recent deed,
>     He dash'd his carbine on the ground."

And then Bothwellhaugh tells his tale of blood, describing the procession from which he had singled out his prey :—

> " ' Dark Morton, girt with many a spear,
>     Murder's foul minion, led the van ;
> And clash'd their broadswords in the rear
>     The wild Macfarlanes' plaided clan.

> " ' Glencairn and stout Parkhead were nigh,
>     Obsequious at their Regent's rein,
> And haggard Lindsay's iron eye,
>     That saw fair Mary weep in vain.

> " ' 'Mid pennon'd spears, a steely grove,
>     Proud Murray's plumage floated high ;
> Scarce could his trampling charger move,
>     So close the minions crowded nigh.

> " ' From the raised vizor's shade, his eye,
>     Dark rolling, glanced the ranks along,
> And his steel truncheon waved on high,
>     Seem'd marshalling the iron throng.

> " ' But yet his sadden'd brow confess'd
>     A passing shade of doubt and awe ;
> Some fiend was whispering in his breast,
>     " Beware of injured Bothwellhaugh ! "

> " ' The death-shot parts,—the charger springs,—
>     Wild rises tumult's startling roar !
> And Murray's plumy helmet rings—
>     Rings on the ground to rise no more.' "

This was the ballad which made so strong an impression on Thomas Campbell, the poet.   Referring to some of the

lines I have quoted, Campbell said,—" I have repeated
them so often on the North Bridge that the whole frater-
nity of coachmen know me by tongue as I pass. To be
sure, to a mind in sober, serious, street-walking humour, it
must bear an appearance of lunacy when one stamps with
the hurried pace and fervent shake of the head which
strong, pithy poetry excites."[1] I suppose anecdotes of
this kind have been oftener told of Scott than of any
other English poet. Indeed, Sir Walter, who understood
himself well, gives the explanation in one of his diaries:—
" I am sensible," he says, " that if there be anything good
about my poetry or prose either, it is a hurried frankness
of composition, which pleases soldiers, sailors, and young
people of bold and active dispositions."[2] He might have
included old people too. I have heard of two old men—
complete strangers—passing each other on a dark London
night, when one of them happened to be repeating to himself, just as Campbell did to the hackney coachmen of the
North Bridge of Edinburgh, the last lines of the account
of Flodden Field in *Marmion*, " Charge, Chester, charge,"
when suddenly a reply came out of the darkness, " On,
Stanley, on," whereupon they finished the death of Marmion between them, took off their hats to each other, and
parted, laughing. Scott's is almost the only poetry
in the English language that not only runs thus in the
head of average men, but heats the head in which it
runs by the mere force of its hurried frankness of
style, to use Scott's own terms, or by that of its strong
and pithy eloquence, as Campbell phrased it. And in
*Cadyow Castle* this style is at its culminating point.

[1] Lockhart's *Life of Scott*, ii. 79.
[2] Lockhart's *Life of Scott*, viii. 370.

## CHAPTER V.

SCOTT'S MATURER POEMS.

SCOTT'S genius flowered late.  *Cadyow Castle,* the first of
his poems, I think, that has indisputable genius plainly
stamped on its terse and fiery lines, was composed in 1802,
when he was already thirty-one years of age.   It was in
the same year that he wrote the first canto of his first
great romance in verse, *The Lay of the Last Minstrel,* a
poem which did not appear till 1805, when he was thirty-
four.   The first canto (not including the framework, of
which the aged harper is the principal figure) was written
in the lodgings to which he was confined for a fortnight
in 1802, by a kick received from a horse on Portobello
sands, during a charge of the Volunteer Cavalry in which
Scott was cornet.   The poem was originally intended to
be included in the *Border Minstrelsy,* as one of the
studies in the antique style, but soon outgrew the limits of
such a study both in length and in the freedom of its
manner.   Both the poorest and the best parts of *The Lay*
were in a special manner due to Lady Dalkeith (afterwards
Duchess of Buccleugh), who suggested it, and in whose
honour the poem was written.   It was she who requested
Scott to write a poem on the legend of the goblin
page, Gilpin Horner, and this Scott attempted,—and,
so far as the goblin himself was concerned, conspicuously

failed. He himself clearly saw that the story of this unmanageable imp was both confused and uninteresting, and that in fact he had to extricate himself from the original groundwork of the tale, as from a regular literary scrape, in the best way he could. In a letter to Miss Seward, Scott says,—" At length the story appeared so uncouth that I was fain to put it into the mouth of my old minstrel, lest the nature of it should be misunderstood, and I should be suspected of setting up a new school of poetry, instead of a feeble attempt to imitate the old. In the process of the romance, the page, intended to be a principal person in the work, contrived (from the baseness of his natural propensities, I suppose) to slink down stairs into the kitchen, and now he must e'en abide there."[1] And I venture to say that no reader of the poem ever has distinctly understood what the goblin page did or did not do, what it was that was "lost" throughout the poem and "found" at the conclusion, what was the object of his personating the young heir of the house of Scott, and whether or not that object was answered ;—what use, if any, the magic book of Michael Scott was to the Lady of Branksome, or whether it was only harm to her ; and I doubt moreover whether any one ever cared an iota what answer, or whether any answer, might be given to any of these questions. All this, as Scott himself clearly perceived, was left confused, and not simply vague. The goblin imp had been more certainly an imp of mischief to him than even to his boyish ancestor. But if Lady Dalkeith suggested the poorest part of the poem, she certainly inspired its best part. Scott says, as we have seen, that he brought in the aged harper to save himself

---

[1] Lockhart's *Life of Scott*, ii. **217.**

from the imputation of "setting up a new school of
poetry" instead of humbly imitating an old school. But
I think that the chivalrous wish to do honour to Lady
Dalkeith, both as a personal friend and as the wife of his
"chief,"—as he always called the head of the house of
Scott,—had more to do with the introduction of the aged
harper, than the wish to guard himself against the imputation of attempting a new poetic style. He clearly
intended the Duchess of *The Lay* to represent the
Countess for whom he wrote it, and the aged harper, with
his reverence and gratitude and self-distrust, was only the
disguise in which he felt that he could best pour out his loyalty, and the romantic devotion with which both Lord and
Lady Dalkeith, but especially the latter, had inspired him.
It was certainly this beautiful framework which assured
the immediate success and permanent charm of the poem;
and the immediate success was for that day something
marvellous. The magnificent quarto edition of 750 copies
was soon exhausted, and an octavo edition of 1500 copies
was sold out within the year. In the following year two
editions, containing together 4250 copies, were disposed
of, and before twenty-five years had elapsed, that is, before
1830, 44,000 copies of the poem had been bought by the
public in this country, taking account of the legitimate
trade alone. Scott gained in all by *The Lay* 769*l.*, an
unprecedented sum in those times for an author to obtain
from any poem. Little more than half a century before,
Johnson received but fifteen guineas for his stately poem
on *The Vanity of Human Wishes,* and but ten guineas for
his *London.* I do not say that Scott's poem had not much
more in it of true poetic fire, though Scott himself, I
believe, preferred these poems of Johnson's to anything
that he himself ever wrote. But the disproportion in

the reward was certainly enormous, and yet what Scott
gained by his *Lay* was of course much less than he
gained by any of his subsequent poems of equal, or anything like equal, length.   Thus for *Marmion* he received
1000 guineas long before the poem was published, and
for *one half* of the copyright of *The Lord of the Isles*
Constable paid Scott 1500 guineas.   If we ask ourselves to
what this vast popularity of Scott's poems, and especially
of the earlier of them (for, as often happens, he was better
remunerated for his later and much inferior poems than
for his earlier and more brilliant productions) is due, I
think the answer must be for the most part, the high
romantic glow and extraordinary romantic simplicity of the
poetical elements they contained.   Take the old harper
of *The Lay*, a figure which arrested the attention of Pitt
during even that last most anxious year of his anxious life,
the year of Ulm and Austerlitz.   The lines in which Scott
describes the old man's embarrassment when first urged
to play, produced on Pitt, according to his own account,
" an effect which I might have expected in painting, but
could never have fancied capable of being given in poetry."[1]
Every one knows the lines to which Pitt refers :—

> " The humble boon was soon obtain'd ;
> The aged minstrel audience gain'd.
> But, when he reach'd the room of state,
> Where she with all her ladies sate,
> Perchance he wish'd his boon denied ;
> For, when to tune the harp he tried,
> His trembling hand had lost the ease
> Which marks security to please ;
> And scenes long past, of joy and pain,
> Came wildering o'er his aged brain,—
> He tried to tune his harp in vain !

[1] Lockhart's *Life of Scott*, ii. 226.

The pitying Duchess praised its chime,
And gave him heart, and gave him time,
Till every string's according glee
Was blended into harmony.
And then, he said, he would full fain
He could recall an ancient strain
He never thought to sing again.
It was not framed for village churls,
But for high dames and mighty earls;
He'd play'd it to King Charles the Good,
When he kept Court at Holyrood;
And much he wish'd, yet fear'd, to try
The long-forgotten melody.
Amid the strings his fingers stray'd,
And an uncertain warbling made,
And oft he shook his hoary head.
But when he caught the measure wild
The old man raised his face, and smiled;
And lighten'd up his faded eye,
With all a poet's ecstasy!
In varying cadence, soft or strong,
He swept the sounding chords along;
The present scene, the future lot,
His toils, his wants, were all forgot;
Cold diffidence and age's frost
In the full tide of song were lost;
Each blank in faithless memory void
The poet's glowing thought supplied;
And, while his harp responsive rung,
'Twas thus the latest minstrel sung.
\*       \*       \*       \*       \*
Here paused the harp; and with its swell
The master's fire and courage fell;
Dejectedly and low he bow'd,
And, gazing timid on the crowd,
He seem'd to seek in every eye
If they approved his minstrelsy;
And, diffident of present praise,
Somewhat he spoke of former days,
And how old age, and wandering long,
Had done his hand and harp some wrong."

These lines hardly illustrate, I think, the particular form
of Mr. Pitt's criticism, for a quick succession of fine
shades of feeling of this kind could never have been
delineated in a painting, or indeed in a series of paintings,
at all, while they *are* so given in the poem. But the
praise itself, if not its exact form, is amply deserved.
The singular depth of the romantic glow in this passage,
and its equally singular simplicity,—a simplicity which
makes it intelligible to every one,—are conspicuous to
every reader. It is not what is called classical poetry, for
there is no severe outline,—no sculptured completeness
and repose,—no satisfying wholeness of effect to the eye
of the mind,—no embodiment of a great action. The poet
gives us a breath, a ripple of alternating fear and hope in
the heart of an old man, and that is all. He catches an
emotion that had its roots deep in the past, and that is
striving onward towards something in the future ;—he
traces the wistfulness and self-distrust with which age seeks
to recover the feelings of youth,—the delight with which it
greets them when they come,—the hesitation and diffidence with which it recalls them as they pass away, and
questions the triumph it has just won, — and he paints all
this without subtlety, without complexity, but with a
swiftness such as few poets ever surpassed. Generally,
however, Scott prefers action itself for his subject, to any
feeling, however active in its bent. The cases in which
he makes a study of any mood of feeling, as he does of
this harper's feeling, are comparatively rare. Deloraine's
night-ride to Melrose is a good deal more in Scott's
ordinary way, than this study of the old harper's wistful
mood. But whatever his subject, his treatment of it
is the same. His lines are always strongly drawn ;
his handling is always simple ; and his subject always

E

romantic. But though romantic, it is simple almost to
bareness,—one of the great causes both of his popularity,
and of that deficiency in his poetry of which so many
of his admirers become conscious when they compare him
with other and richer poets. Scott used to say that in
poetry Byron " bet " him ; and no doubt that in which
chiefly as a poet he " bet " him, was in the variety, the
richness, the lustre of his effects. A certain ruggedness
and bareness was of the essence of Scott's idealism and
romance. It was so in relation to scenery. He told
Washington Irving that he loved the very nakedness of
the Border country. " It has something," he said, " bold
and stern and solitary about it. When I have been for
some time in the rich scenery about Edinburgh, which
is like ornamented garden-land, I begin to wish myself
back again among my honest grey hills, and if I did not
see the heather at least once a year, *I think I should die.*" [1]
Now, the bareness which Scott so loved in his native
scenery, there is in all his romantic elements of feeling.
It is while he is bold and stern, that he is at his highest
ideal point. Directly he begins to attempt rich or pretty
subjects, as in parts of *The Lady of the Lake*, and a good
deal of *The Lord of the Isle*s, and still more in *The Bridal
of Triermain*, his charm disappears. It is in painting
those moods and exploits, in relation to which Scott
shares most completely the feelings of ordinary men, but
experiences them with far greater strength and purity
than ordinary men, that he triumphs as a poet. Mr.
Lockhart tells us that some of Scott's senses were decidedly " blunt," and one seems to recognize this in the
simplicity of his romantic effects. " It is a fact," he says,

---

[1] Lockhart's *Life of Scott*, v. 248.

"which some philosophers may think worth setting
down, that Scott's organization, as to more than one of
the senses, was the reverse of exquisite.  He had very
little of what musicians call an ear; his smell was hardly
more delicate.  I have seen him stare about, quite unconscious of the cause, when his whole company betrayed
their uneasiness at the approach of an overkept haunch
of venison ; and neither by the nose nor the palate could
he distinguish corked wine from sound.  He could never
tell Madeira from sherry,—nay, an Oriental friend
having sent him a butt of *sheeraz*, when he remembered
the circumstance some time afterwards and called for a
bottle to have Sir John Malcolm's opinion of its quality,
it turned out that his butler, mistaking the label, had
already served up half the bin as *sherry*.  Port he considered as physic . . . . in truth he liked no wines
except sparkling champagne and claret ; but even as to
the last he was no connoisseur, and sincerely preferred a
tumbler of whisky-toddy to the most precious 'liquid-
ruby' that ever flowed in the cup of a prince." [1]

However, Scott's eye was very keen :—"*It was commonly him,*" as his little son once said, "*that saw the
hare sitting.*"  And his perception of colour was very
delicate as well as his mere sight.  As Mr. Ruskin has
pointed out, his landscape painting is almost all done by
the lucid use of colour.  Nevertheless this bluntness
of organization in relation to the less important senses,
no doubt contributed something to the singleness and simplicity of the deeper and more vital of Scott's romantic
impressions ; at least there is good reason to suppose that
delicate and complicated susceptibilities do at least

[1] Lockhart's *Life of Scott*, v. 338.

E 2

diminish the chance of living a strong and concentrated life—do risk the frittering away of feeling on the mere backwaters of sensations, even if they do not directly tend towards artificial and indirect forms of character. Scott's romance is like his native scenery,—bold, bare and rugged, with a swift deep stream of strong pure feeling running through it. There is plenty of colour in his pictures, as there is on the Scotch hills when the heather is out. And so too there is plenty of intensity in his romantic situations; but it is the intensity of simple, natural, unsophisticated, hardy, and manly characters. But as for subtleties and fine shades of feeling in his poems, or anything like the manifold harmonies of the richer arts, they are not to be found, or, if such complicated shading is to be found—and it is perhaps attempted in some faint measure in *The Bridal of Triermain*, the poem in which Scott tried to pass himself off for Erskine,—it is only at the expense of the higher qualities of his romantic poetry, that even in this small measure it is supplied. Again, there is no rich music in his verse. It is its rapid onset, its hurrying strength, which so fixes it in the mind.

It was not till 1808, three years after the publication of *The Lay*, that *Marmion*, Scott's greatest poem, was published. But I may as well say what seems necessary of that and his other poems, while I am on the subject of his poetry. *Marmion* has all the advantage over *The Lay of the Last Minstrel* that a coherent story told with force and fulness, and concerned with the same class of subjects as *The Lay*, must have over a confused and ill-managed legend, the only original purpose of which was to serve as the opportunity for a picture of Border life and strife. Scott's poems have sometimes been depreciated as mere

*novelettes* in verse, and I think that some of them may be
more or less liable to this criticism.  For instance, *The
Lady of the Lake,* with the exception of two or three
brilliant passages, has always seemed to me more of a ver-
sified *novelette,*—without the higher and broader character-
istics of Scott's prose novels—than of a poem.  I suppose
what one expects from a poem as distinguished from a
romance—even though the poem incorporates a story—is
that it should not rest for its chief interest on the mere
development of the story ; but rather that the narrative
should be quite subordinate to that insight into the deeper
side of life and manners, in expressing which poetry has
so great an advantage over prose.  Of *The Lay* and *Marmion* this is true ; less true of *The Lady of the Lake,* and
still less of *Rokeby,* or *The Lord of the Isles,* and this is
why *The Lay* and *Marmion* seem so much superior as
poems to the others.  They lean less on the interest of
mere incident, more on that of romantic feeling and the
great social and historic features of the day.  *Marmion* was
composed in great part in the saddle, and the stir of a
charge of cavalry seems to be at the very core of it.
" For myself," said Scott, writing to a lady correspondent
at a time when he was in active service as a volunteer, " I
must own that to one who has, like myself, *la tête un peu
exaltée,* the pomp and circumstance of war gives, for a
time, a very poignant and pleasing sensation." [1]  And you
feel this all through *Marmion* even more than in *The Lay.*
Mr. Darwin would probably say that Auld Wat of Harden had about as much responsibility for *Marmion* as Sir
Walter himself.  " You will expect," he wrote to the same
lady, who was personally unknown to him at that time,

---

[1] Lockhart's *Life of Scott,* ii. 137.

"to see a person who had dedicated himself to literary pursuits, and you will find me a rattle-skulled, half-lawyer, half-sportsman, through whose head a regiment of horse has been exercising since he was five years old."[1] And what Scott himself felt in relation to the martial elements of his poetry, soldiers in the field felt with equal force. "In the course of the day when *The Lady of the Lake* first reached Sir Adam Fergusson, he was posted with his company on a point of ground exposed to the enemy's artillery, somewhere no doubt on the lines of Torres Vedras. The men were ordered to lie prostrate on the ground; while they kept that attitude, the captain, kneeling at the head, read aloud the description of the battle in Canto VI., and the listening soldiers only interrupted him by a joyous huzza when the French shot struck the bank close above them."[2] It is not often that martial poetry has been put to such a test; but we can well understand with what rapture a Scotch force lying on the ground to shelter from the French fire, would enter into such passages as the following:—

"Their light-arm'd archers far and near
    Survey'd the tangled ground,
Their centre ranks, with pike and spear,
    A twilight forest frown'd,
Their barbèd horsemen, in the rear,
    The stern battalia crown'd.
No cymbal clash'd, no clarion rang,
    Still were the pipe and drum;
Save heavy tread, and armour's clang,
    The sullen march was dumb.
There breathed no wind their crests to shake,
    Or wave their flags abroad;
Scarce the frail aspen seem'd to quake,
    That shadow'd o'er their road.

[1] Lockhart's *Life of Scott*, ii. 259.
[2] Lockhart's *Life of Scott*, iii. 327.

Their vanward scouts no tidings bring,
    Can rouse no lurking foe,
Nor spy a trace of living thing
    Save when they stirr'd the roe ;
The host moves like a deep-sea wave,
Where rise no rocks its power to brave,
    High-swelling, dark, and slow.
The lake is pass'd, and now they gain
A narrow and a broken plain,
Before the Trosach's rugged jaws,
And here the horse and spearmen pause,
While, to explore the dangerous glen,
Dive through the pass the archer-men.

" At once there rose so wild a yell
Within that dark and narrow dell,
As all the fiends from heaven that fell
Had peal'd the banner-cry of Hell !
    Forth from the pass, in tumult driven,
    Like chaff before the wind of heaven,
        The archery appear ;
    For life ! for life ! their plight they ply,
    And shriek, and shout, and battle-cry,
    And plaids and bonnets waving high,
    And broadswords flashing to the sky,
        Are maddening in the rear.
Onward they drive, in dreadful race,
    Pursuers and pursued ;
Before that tide of flight and chase,
How shall it keep its rooted place,
    The spearmen's twilight wood ?
Down, down, cried Mar, ' your lances down
    Bear back both friend and foe ! '
Like reeds before the tempest's frown,
That serried grove of lances brown
    At once lay levell'd low ;
And, closely shouldering side to side,
The bristling ranks the onset bide,—
' We'll quell the savage mountaineer,
    As their Tinchel cows the game !
They came as fleet as forest deer,
    We'll drive them back as tame.' "

But admirable in its stern and deep excitement as
that is, the battle of Flodden in *Marmion* passes it in
vigour, and constitutes perhaps the most perfect description of war by one who was—almost—both poet and
warrior, which the English language contains.

And *Marmion* registers the high-water mark of Scott's
poetical power, not only in relation to the painting of
war, but in relation to the painting of nature.  Critics
from the beginning onwards have complained of the
six introductory epistles, as breaking the unity of the
story.  But I cannot see that the remark has weight.  No
poem is written for those who read it as they do a novel—
merely to follow the interest of the story ; or if any poem
be written for such readers, it deserves to die.  On such
a principle—which treats a poem as a mere novel and
nothing else,—you might object to Homer that he in-
terrupts the battle so often to dwell on the origin of
the heroes who are waging it ; or to Byron that he
deserts Childe Harold to meditate on the rapture of
solitude.  To my mind the ease and frankness of these
confessions of the author's recollections give a picture
of his life and character while writing *Marmion*,
which adds greatly to its attraction as a poem.  You
have a picture at once not only of the scenery, but of
the mind in which that scenery is mirrored, and are
brought back frankly, at fit intervals, from the one to the
other, in the mode best adapted to help you to appreciate
the relation of the poet to the poem.  At least if
Milton's various interruptions of a much more ambitious
theme, to muse upon his own qualifications or disqualifi-
cations for the task he had attempted, be not artistic
mistakes—and I never heard of any one who thought
them so—I cannot see any reason why Scott's periodic

recurrence to his own personal history should be artistic mistakes either. If Scott's reverie was less lofty than Milton's, so also was his story. It seems to me as fitting to describe the relation between the poet and his theme in the one case as in the other. What can be more truly a part of *Marmion*, as a poem, though not as a story, than that introduction to the first canto in which Scott expresses his passionate sympathy with the high national feeling of the moment, in his tribute to Pitt and Fox, and then reproaches himself for attempting so great a subject and returns to what he calls his "rude legend," the very essence of which was, however, a passionate appeal to the spirit of national independence? What can be more germane to the poem than the delineation of the strength the poet had derived from musing in the bare and rugged solitudes of St. Mary's Lake, in the introduction to the second canto? Or than the striking auto-biographical study of his own infancy which I have before extracted from the introduction to the third? It seems to me that *Marmion* without these introductions would be like the hills which border Yarrow, without the stream and lake in which they are reflected.

Never at all events in any later poem was Scott's touch as a mere painter so terse and strong. What a picture of a Scotch winter is given in these few lines :—

> "The sheep before the pinching heaven
> To shelter'd dale and down are driven,
> Where yet some faded herbage pines,
> And yet a watery sunbeam shines :
> In meek despondency they eye
> The wither'd sward and wintry sky,
> And from beneath their summer hill
> Stray sadly by Glenkinnon's rill."

Again, if Scott is ever Homeric (which I cannot think

he often is, in spite of Sir Francis Doyle's able criticism,—
(he is too short, too sharp, and too eagerly bent on his
rugged way, for a poet who is always delighting to find
loopholes, even in battle, from which to look out upon the
great story of human nature), he is certainly nearest to
it in such a passage as this :—

> " The Isles-men carried at their backs
> The ancient Danish battle-axe.
> They raised a wild and wondering cry
> As with his guide rode Marmion by.
> Loud were their clamouring tongues, as when
> The clanging sea-fowl leave the fen,
> And, with their cries discordant mix'd,
> Grumbled and yell'd the pipes betwixt."

In hardly any of Scott's poetry do we find much of
what is called the *curiosa felicitas* of expression,—the
magic use of *words*, as distinguished from the mere general
effect of vigour, purity, and concentration of purpose.
But in *Marmion* occasionally we do find such a use.
Take this description, for instance, of the Scotch tents
near Edinburgh :—

> " A thousand did I say ?  I ween
> Thousands on thousands there were seen,
> That chequer'd all the heath between
>    The streamlet and the town ;
> In crossing ranks extending far,
> Forming a camp irregular ;
> Oft giving way where still there stood
> Some relics of the old oak wood,
> That darkly huge did intervene,
> *And tamed the glaring white with green ;*
> In these extended lines there lay
> A martial kingdom's vast array."

The line I have italicized seems to me to have more of
the poet's special magic of expression than is at all usual

with Scott.   The conception of the peaceful green oak-
wood *taming* the glaring white of the tented field, is as
fine in idea as it is in relation to the effect of the mere
colour on the eye.   Judge Scott's poetry by whatever test
you will—whether it be a test of that which is peculiar
to it, its glow of national feeling, its martial ardour, its
swift and rugged simplicity, or whether it be a test of
that which is common to it with most other poetry, its
attraction for all romantic excitements, its special feeling
for the pomp and circumstance of war, its love of light
and colour—and tested either way, *Marmion* will remain
his finest poem.   The battle of Flodden Field touches his
highest point in its expression of stern patriotic feeling,
in its passionate love of daring, and in the force and
swiftness of its movement, no less than in the brilliancy
of its romantic interests, the charm of its picturesque
detail, and the glow of its scenic colouring.   No poet ever
equalled Scott in the description of wild and simple scenes
and the expression of wild and simple feelings.   But I
have said enough now of his poetry, in which, good as it
is, Scott's genius did not reach its highest point.   The
hurried tramp of his somewhat monotonous metre, is apt
to weary the ears of men who do not find their sufficient
happiness, as he did, in dreaming of the wild and daring
enterprises of his loved Border-land.   The very quality
in his verse which makes it seize so powerfully on the
imaginations of plain, bold, adventurous men, often makes
it hammer fatiguingly against the brain of those who
need the relief of a wider horizon and a richer world.

## CHAPTER VI.

### COMPANIONS AND FRIENDS.

I HAVE anticipated in some degree, in speaking of Scott's later poetical works, what, in point of time at least, should follow some slight sketch of his chosen companions, and of his occupations in the first period of his married life. Scott's most intimate friend for some time after he went to college, probably the one who most stimulated his imagination in his youth, and certainly one of his most intimate friends to the very last, was William Clerk, who was called to the bar on the same day as Scott. He was the son of John Clerk of Eldin, the author of a book of some celebrity in its time on *Naval Tactics*. Even in the earliest days of this intimacy, the lads who had been Scott's fellow-apprentices in his father's office, saw with some jealousy his growing friendship with William Clerk, and remonstrated with Scott on the decline of his regard for them, but only succeeded in eliciting from him one of those outbursts of peremptory frankness which anything that he regarded as an attempt to encroach on his own interior liberty of choice always provoked. " I will never cut any man," he said, " unless I detect him in scoundrelism, but I know not what right any of you have to interfere with my choice of my company. As it is, I fairly own that though I like many of you very much, and

have long done so, I think William Clerk well worth you
all put together." [1]    Scott never lost the friendship which
began with this eager enthusiasm, but his chief intimacy
with Clerk was during his younger days.

In 1808 Scott describes Clerk as "a man of the most
acute intellects and powerful apprehension, who, if he
should ever shake loose the fetters of indolence by which
he has been hitherto trammelled, cannot fail to be distinguished in the highest degree."    Whether for the reason
suggested, or for some other, Clerk never actually gained any
other distinction so great as his friendship with Scott conferred upon him.    Probably Scott had discerned the true
secret of his friend's comparative obscurity.    Even while
preparing for the bar, when they had agreed to go
on alternate mornings to each other's lodgings to read
together, Scott found it necessary to modify the arrangement by always visiting his friend, whom he usually found
in bed.    It was William Clerk who sat for the picture of
Darsie Latimer, the hero of *Redgauntlet*,— whence we
should suppose him to have been a lively, generous, susceptible, contentious, and rather helter-skelter young man,
much alive to the ludicrous in all situations, very eager to
see life in all its phases, and somewhat vain of his power
of adapting himself equally to all these phases.    Scott
tells a story of Clerk's being once baffled—almost for the
first time—by a stranger in a stage coach, who would not,
or could not, talk to him on any subject, until at last
Clerk addressed to him this stately remonstrance, "I
have talked to you, my friend, on all the ordinary subjects
—literature, farming, merchandise, gaming, game-laws,
horse-races, suits-at-law, politics, swindling, blasphemy,

---

[1] Lockhart's *Life of Scott*, i. 214.

and philosophy,—is there any one subject that you will favour me by opening upon?" "Sir," replied the inscrutable stranger, "can you say anything clever about '*bend-leather?*"[1] No doubt this superficial familiarity with a vast number of subjects was a great fascination to Scott, and a great stimulus to his own imagination. To the last he held the same opinion of his friend's latent powers. "To my thinking," he wrote in his diary in 1825, "I never met a man of greater powers, of more complete information on all desirable subjects." But in youth at least Clerk seems to have had what Sir Walter calls a characteristic Edinburgh complaint, the "itch for disputation," and though he softened this down in later life, he had always that slight contentiousness of bias which enthusiastic men do not often heartily like, and which may have prevented Scott from continuing to the full the close intimacy of those earlier years. Yet almost his last record of a really delightful evening, refers to a bachelor's dinner given by Mr. Clerk, who remained unmarried, as late as 1827, after all Sir Walter's worst troubles had come upon him. "In short," says the diary, "we really laughed, and real laughter is as rare as real tears. I must say, too, there was a *heart*, a kindly feeling prevailed over the party. Can London give such a dinner?"[2] It is clear ,then, that Clerk's charm for his friend survived to the last, and that it was not the mere inexperience of boyhood, which made Scott esteem him so highly in his early days.

If Clerk pricked, stimulated, and sometimes badgered Scott, another of his friends who became more and more intimate with him, as life went on, and who died before him, always

---

[1] Lockhart's *Life of Scott*, iii. 344.
[2] Lockhart's *Life of Scott*, ix. 75.

soothed him, partly by his gentleness, partly by his almost
feminine dependence.  This was William Erskine, also a
barrister, and son of an Episcopalian clergyman in Perthshire,
—to whose influence it is probably due that Scott himself
always read the English Church service in his own country
house, and does not appear to have retained the Pres-
byterianism into which he was born.  Erskine, who was
afterwards raised to the Bench as Lord Kinnedder—a distinction which he did not survive for many months—was
a good classic, a man of fine, or, as some of his companions thought, of almost superfine taste.  The style
apparently for which he had credit must have been a somewhat mimini-pimini style, if we may judge by Scott's
attempt in *The Bridal of Triermain*, to write in a manner
which he intended to be attributed to his friend.
Erskine was left a widower in middle life, and Scott used
to accuse him of philandering with pretty women,—a
mode of love-making which Scott certainly contrived to
render into verse, in painting Arthur's love-making to
Lucy in that poem.  It seems that some absolutely false
accusation brought against Lord Kinnedder, of an intrigue
with a lady with whom he had been thus philandering,
broke poor Erskine's heart, during his first year as a Judge.
"The Counsellor (as Scott always called him) was,"
says Mr. Lockhart, "a little man of feeble make, who
seemed unhappy when his pony got beyond a footpace,
and had never, I should suppose, addicted himself to any
out of door's sports whatever.  He would, I fancy, as soon
have thought of slaying his own mutton as of handling a
fowling-piece ; he used to shudder when he saw a party
equipped for coursing, as if murder was in the wind ; but
the cool, meditative angler was in his eyes the abomination
of abominations.  His small elegant features, hectic cheek

and soft hazel eyes, were the index of the quick, sensitive, gentle spirit within." "He would dismount to lead his horse down what his friend hardly perceived to be a descent at all; grew pale at a precipice; and, unlike the white lady of Avenel, would go a long way round for a bridge." He shrank from general society, and lived in closer intimacies, and his intimacy with Scott was of the closest. He was Scott's confidant in all literary matters, and his advice was oftener followed on questions of style and form, and of literary enterprise, than that of any other of Scott's friends. It is into Erskine's mouth that Scott puts the supposed exhortation to himself to choose more classical subjects for his poems:—

> " ' Approach those masters o'er whose tomb
> Immortal laurels ever bloom;
> Instructive of the feebler bard,
> Still from the grave their voice is heard;
> From them, and from the paths they show'd,
> Choose honour'd guide and practised road;
> Nor ramble on through brake and maze,
> With harpers rude of barbarous days."

And it is to Erskine that Scott replies,—

> " For me, thus nurtured, dost thou ask
> The classic poet's well-conn'd task?
> Nay, Erskine, nay,—on the wild hill
> Let the wild heath-bell flourish still;
> Cherish the tulip, prune the vine,
> But freely let the woodbine twine,
> And leave untrimm'd the eglantine:
> Nay, my friend, nay,—since oft thy praise
> Hath given fresh vigour to my lays;
> Since oft thy judgment could refine
> My flatten'd thought or cumbrous line,
> Still kind, as is thy wont, attend,
> And in the minstrel spare the friend!"

It was Erskine, too, as Scott expressly states in his

introduction to the *Chronicles of the Canongate*, who reviewed with far too much partiality the *Tales of my Landlord*, in the *Quarterly Review*, for January, 1817,—a review unjustifiably included among Scott's own critical essays, on the very insufficient ground that the MS. reached Murray in Scott's own handwriting. There can, however, be no doubt at all that Scott copied out his friend's MS., in order to increase the mystification which he so much enjoyed as to the authorship of his variously named series of tales. Possibly enough, too, he may have drawn Erskine's attention to the evidence which justified his sketch of the Puritans in *Old Mortality*, evidence which he certainly intended at one time to embody in a reply of his own to the adverse criticism on that book. But though Erskine was Scott's *alter ego* for literary purposes, it is certain that Erskine, with his fastidious, not to say finical, sense of honour, would never have lent his name to cover a puff written by Scott of his own works. A man who, in Scott's own words, died "a victim to a hellishly false story, or rather, I should say, to the sensibility of his own nature, which could not endure even the shadow of reproach,—like the ermine, which is said to pine if its fur is soiled," was not the man to father a puff, even by his dearest friend, on that friend's own creations. Erskine was indeed almost feminine in his love of Scott; but he was feminine with all the irritable and scrupulous delicacy of a man who could not derogate from his own ideal of right, even to serve a friend.

Another friend of Scott's earlier days was John Leyden, Scott's most efficient coadjutor in the collection of the *Border Minstrelsy*,—that eccentric genius, marvellous linguist, and good-natured bear, who, bred a shepherd in one of the wildest valleys of Roxburghshire, had accumulated

F

before the age of nineteen an amount of learning which
confounded the Edinburgh Professors, and who, without
any previous knowledge of medicine, prepared himself to
pass an examination for the medical profession, at six
months' notice of the offer of an assistant-surgeoncy in the
East India Company. It was Leyden who once walked
between forty and fifty miles and back, for the sole purpose of visiting an old person who possessed a copy of a
border ballad that was wanting for the *Minstrelsy*. Scott
was sitting at dinner one day with company, when he
heard a sound at a distance, "like that of the whistling of
a tempest through the torn rigging of a vessel which scuds
before it. The sounds increased as they approached more
near; and Leyden (to the great astonishment of such of
the guests as did not know him) burst into the room
chanting the desiderated ballad with the most enthusiastic
gesture, and all the energy of what he used to call the
*saw-tones* of his voice."[1] Leyden's great antipathy was
Ritson, an ill-conditioned antiquarian, of vegetarian principles, whom Scott alone of all the antiquarians of that
day could manage to tame and tolerate. In Scott's
absence one day, during his early married life at Lasswade, Mrs. Scott inadvertently offered Ritson a slice of beef,
when that strange man burst out in such outrageous tones
at what he chose to suppose an insult, that Leyden threatened to "thraw his neck" if he were not silent, a threat
which frightened Ritson out of the cottage. On another
occasion, simply in order to tease Ritson, Leyden complained that the meat was overdone, and sent to the
kitchen for a plate of literally raw beef, and ate it up
solely for the purpose of shocking his crazy rival in anti-

[1] Lockhart's *Life of Scott*, ii. 56.

quarian research.   Poor Leyden did not long survive his
experience of the Indian climate.   And with him died a
passion for knowledge of a very high order, combined
with no inconsiderable poetical gifts.   It was in the study
of such eccentric beings as Leyden that Scott doubtless
acquired his taste for painting the humours of Scotch
character.

Another wild shepherd, and wilder genius among Scott's
associates, not only in those earlier days, but to the end, was
that famous Ettrick Shepherd, James Hogg, who was
always quarrelling with his brother poet, as far as Scott permitted it, and making it up again when his better feelings
returned.   In a shepherd's dress, and with hands fresh
from sheep-shearing, he came to dine for the first time with
Scott in Castle Street, and finding Mrs. Scott lying on the
sofa, immediately stretched himself at full length on another sofa ; for, as he explained afterwards, "I thought I
could not do better than to imitate the lady of the house."
At dinner, as the wine passed, he advanced from "Mr. Scott,"
to "Shirra" (Sheriff), "Scott," "Walter," and finally
"Wattie," till at supper he convulsed every one by addressing Mrs. Scott familiarly as "Charlotte." [1]   Hogg wrote
certain short poems, the beauty of which in their kind
Sir Walter himself never approached ; but he was a man
almost without self-restraint or self-knowledge, though
he had a great deal of self-importance, and hardly knew
how much he owed to Scott's magnanimous and ever-
forbearing kindness, or if he did, felt the weight of gratitude a burden on his heart.   Very different was William
Laidlaw, a farmer on the banks of the Yarrow, always Scott's
friend, and afterwards his manager at Abbotsford, through

[1] Lockhart's *Life of Scott*, ii. 168-9.

whose hand he dictated many of his novels.   Mr. Laidlaw
was one of Scott's humbler friends,—a class of friends
with whom he seems always to have felt more completely
at his ease than any others—who gave at least as much as
he received, one of those wise, loyal, and thoughtful men
in a comparatively modest position of life, whom Scott
delighted to trust, and never trusted without finding his
trust justified.   In addition to these Scotch friends, Scott
had made, even before the publication of his *Border Minstrelsy*, not a few in London or its neighbourhood,—of
whom the most important at this time was the grey-eyed,
hatchet-faced, courteous George Ellis, as Leyden described
him, the author of various works on ancient English poetry
and romance, who combined with a shrewd, satirical vein,
and a great knowledge of the world, political as well as
literary, an exquisite taste in poetry, and a warm heart.
Certainly Ellis's criticism on his poems was the truest and
best that Scott ever received ; and had he lived to read his
novels,—only one of which was published before Ellis's
death,—he might have given Scott more useful help than
either Ballantyne or even Erskine.

## CHAPTER VII.

### FIRST COUNTRY HOMES.

So completely was Scott by nature an out-of-doors man that he cannot be adequately known either through his poems or through his friends, without also knowing his external surroundings and occupations.   His first country home was the cottage at Lasswade, on the Esk, about six miles from Edinburgh, which he took in 1798, a few months after his marriage, and retained till 1804.   It was a pretty little cottage, in the beautification of which Scott felt great pride, and where he exercised himself in the small beginnings of those tastes for altering and planting which grew so rapidly upon him, and at last enticed him into castle-building and tree-culture on a dangerous, not to say, ruinous scale.   One of Scott's intimate friends, the master of Rokeby, by whose house and neighbourhood the poem of that name was suggested, Mr. Morritt, walked along the Esk in 1808 with Scott four years after he had left it, and was taken out of his way to see it.   " I have been bringing you," he said, "where there is little enough to be seen, only that Scotch cottage, but though not worth looking at, I could not pass it.   It was our first country house when newly married, and many a contrivance it had to make it comfortable.   I made a dining-table for it with my own hands.   Look at these two miserable willow-trees

on either side the gate into the enclosure ; they are tied
together at the top to be an arch, and a cross made of two
sticks over them is not yet decayed.   To be sure it is not
much of a lion to show a stranger ; but I wanted to see it
again myself, for I assure you that after I had constructed
it, *mamma* (Mrs. Scott) and I both of us thought it so fine,
we turned out to see it by moonlight, and walked back-
wards from it to the cottage-door, in admiration of our own
magnificence and its picturesque effect." It was here at Lasswade that he bought the phaeton, which was the first
wheeled carriage that ever penetrated to Liddesdale, a feat
which it accomplished in the first August of this century.

When Scott left the cottage at Lasswade in 1804, it was
to take up his country residence in Selkirkshire, of which
he had now been made sheriff, in a beautiful little house
belonging to his cousin, Major-General Sir James Russell,
and known to all the readers of Scott's poetry as the
Ashestiel of the *Marmion* introductions.   The Glenkinnon
brook dashes in a deep ravine through the grounds to join
the Tweed ; behind the house rise the hills which divide
the Tweed from the Yarrow ; and an easy ride took Scott
into the scenery of the Yarrow.   The description of
Ashestiel, and the brook which runs through it, in the
introduction to the first canto of *Marmion* is indeed one
of the finest specimens of Scott's descriptive poetry :—

> "November's sky is chill and drear,
> November's leaf is red and sear ;
> Late, gazing down the steepy linn,
> That hems our little garden in,
> Low in its dark and narrow glen,
> You scarce the rivulet might ken,
> So thick the tangled greenwood grew,
> So feeble trill'd the streamlet through ;
> Now, murmuring hoarse, and frequent seen,
> Through bush and briar no longer green,

> An angry brook, it sweeps the glade,
> Brawls over rock and wild cascade,
> And, foaming brown with doubled speed,
> Hurries its waters to the Tweed."

Selkirk was his nearest town, and that was seven miles from Ashestiel; and even his nearest neighbour was at Yair, a few miles off lower down the Tweed, — Yair of which he wrote in another of the introductions to *Marmion* :—

> " From Yair, which hills so closely bind
> Scarce can the Tweed his passage find,
> Though much he fret, and chafe, and toil,
> Till all his eddying currents boil."

At Ashestiel it was one of his greatest delights to look after his relative's woods, and to dream of planting and thinning woods of his own, a dream only too amply realized. It was here that a new kitchen-range was sunk for some time in the ford, which was so swollen by a storm in 1805 that the horse and cart that brought it were themselves with difficulty rescued from the waters. And it was here that Scott first entered on that active life of literary labour in close conjunction with an equally active life of rural sport, which gained him a well-justified reputation as the hardest worker and the heartiest player in the kingdom. At Lasswade Scott's work had been done at night; but serious headaches made him change his habit at Ashestiel, and rise steadily at five, lighting his own fire in winter. " Arrayed in his shooting-jacket, or whatever dress he meant to use till dinner-time, he was seated at his desk by six o'clock, all his papers arranged before him in the most accurate order, and his books of reference marshalled around him on the floor, while at least one favourite dog lay watching his eye, just beyond the line

of circumvallation. Thus, by the time the family assembled
for breakfast, between nine and ten, he had done enough,
in his own language, 'to break the neck of the day's work.'
After breakfast a couple of hours more were given to his
solitary tasks, and by noon he was, as he used to say, his
'own man.' When the weather was bad, he would labour
incessantly all the morning; but the general rule was to be
out and on horseback by one o'clock at the latest; while,
if any more distant excursion had been proposed overnight,
he was ready to start on it by ten; his occasional rainy
days of unintermitted study, forming, as he said, a fund
in his favour, out of which he was entitled to draw for
accommodation whenever the sun shone with special brightness." In his earlier days none of his horses liked to be
fed except by their master. When Brown Adam was
saddled, and the stable-door opened, the horse would trot
round to the leaping-on stone of his own accord, to be
mounted, and was quite intractable under any one but
Scott. Scott's life might well be fairly divided—just as
history is divided into reigns—by the succession of
his horses and dogs. The reigns of Captain, Lieutenant, Brown Adam, Daisy, divide at least the
period up to Waterloo; while the reigns of Sybil
Grey, and the Covenanter, or Douce Davie, divide the
period of Scott's declining years. During the brilliant
period of the earlier novels we hear less of Scott's horses;
but of his deerhounds there is an unbroken succession.
Camp, Maida (the "Bevis" of *Woodstock*), and Nimrod, reigned successively between Sir Walter's marriage
and his death. It was Camp on whose death he relin-
quished a dinner invitation previously accepted, on the
ground that the death of "an old friend" rendered him
unwilling to dine out; Maida to whom he erected a marble

monument, and Nimrod of whom he spoke so affect-
ingly as too good a dog for his diminished fortunes during
his absence in Italy on the last hopeless journey.

Scott's amusements at Ashestiel, besides riding, in which
he was fearless to rashness, and coursing, which was the
chief form of sporting in the neighbourhood, comprehended
"burning the water," as salmon-spearing by torchlight was
called, in the course of which he got many a ducking. Mr.
Skene gives an amusing picture of their excursions together
from Ashestiel among the hills, he himself followed by
a lanky Savoyard, and Scott by a portly Scotch butler
—both servants alike highly sensitive as to their personal
dignity—on horses which neither of the attendants could
sit well. "Scott's heavy lumbering buffetier had provided himself against the mountain storms with a huge
cloak, which, when the cavalcade was at gallop, streamed
at full stretch from his shoulders, and kept flapping in the
other's face, who, having more than enough to do in pre-
serving his own equilibrium, could not think of attempting
at any time to control the pace of his steed, and had no
relief but fuming and *pesting* at the *sacré manteau*, in
language happily unintelligible to its wearer. Now and
then some ditch or turf-fence rendered it indispensable to
adventure on a leap, and no farce could have been more
amusing than the display of politeness which then occurred
between these worthy equestrians, each courteously declining in favour of his friend the honour of the first experiment, the horses fretting impatient beneath them, and
the dogs clamouring encouragement."[1] Such was Scott's
order of life at Ashestiel, where he remained from 1804
to 1812. As to his literary work here, it was enormous.

[1] Lockhart's *Life of Scott*, ii. 268-9.

Besides finishing *The Lay of the Last Minstrel*, writing
*Marmion*, *The Lady of the Lake*, part of *The Bridal
of Triermain*, and part of *Rokeby*, and writing reviews,
he wrote a *Life of Dryden*, and edited his works anew
with some care, in eighteen volumes, edited *Somers's Collection of Tracts*, in thirteen volumes, quarto, *Sir Ralph
Sadler's Life, Letters, and State Papers*, in three volumes,
quarto, *Miss Seward's Life and Poetical Works*, *The Secret
History of the Court of James I.*, in two volumes, *Strutt's
Queenhoo Hall*, in four volumes, 12mo., and various other
single volumes, and began his heavy work on the edition
of Swift.    This was the literary work of eight years,
during which he had the duties of his Sheriffship, and,
after he gave up his practice as a barrister, the duties of
his Deputy Clerkship of Session to discharge regularly.
The editing of Dryden alone would have seemed to most
men of leisure a pretty full occupation for these eight
years, and though I do not know that Scott edited
with the anxious care with which that sort of work is
often now prepared, that he went into all the arguments
for a doubtful reading with the pains that Mr. Dyce spent
on the various readings of Shakespeare, or that Mr.
Spedding spent on a various reading of Bacon, yet Scott
did his work in a steady, workmanlike manner, which
satisfied the most fastidious critics of that day, and he was
never, I believe, charged with hurrying or scamping it.
His biographies of Swift and Dryden are plain solid pieces
of work—not exactly the works of art which biographies
have been made in our day—not comparable to Carlyle's
studies of Cromwell or Frederick, or, in point of art, even
to the life of John Sterling, but still sensible and interesting,
sound in judgment, and animated in style.

## CHAPTER VIII.

REMOVAL TO ABBOTSFORD, AND LIFE THERE.

In May, 1812, Scott having now at last obtained the salary
of the Clerkship of Session, the work of which he had for
more than five years discharged without pay, indulged himself in realizing his favourite dream of buying a "mountain
farm" at Abbotsford,—five miles lower down the Tweed
than his cottage at Ashestiel, which was now again
claimed by the family of Russell,—and migrated thither
with his household gods. The children long remembered
the leave-taking as one of pure grief, for the villagers
were much attached both to Scott and to his wife, who
had made herself greatly beloved by her untiring goodness
to the sick among her poor neighbours. But Scott himself describes the migration as a scene in which their
neighbours found no small share of amusement. " Our
flitting and removal from Ashestiel baffled all description ;
we had twenty-five cartloads of the veriest trash in nature,
besides dogs, pigs, ponies, poultry, cows, calves, bare-
headed wenches, and bare-breeched boys." [1]

To another friend Scott wrote that the neighbours had
"been much delighted with the procession of my furni-
ture, in which old swords, bows, targets, and lances, made
a very conspicuous show. A family of turkeys was

[1] Lockhart's *Life of Scott*, iv. 6.

accommodated within the helmet of some *preux chevalier*
of ancient border fame; and the very cows, for aught I
know, were bearing banners and muskets. I assure your
ladyship that this caravan attended by a dozen of ragged
rosy peasant children, carrying fishing-rods and spears,
and leading ponies, greyhounds, and spaniels, would, as
it crossed the Tweed, have furnished no bad subject for
the pencil, and really reminded me of one of the gipsy
groups of Callot upon their march." [1]

The place thus bought for 4000*l*.,—half of which, according to Scott's bad and sanguine habit, was borrowed
from his brother, and half raised on the security of a poem
at the moment of sale wholly unwritten, and not completed even when he removed to Abbotsford—"Rokeby"
—became only too much of an idol for the rest of Scott's
life. Mr. Lockhart admits that before the crash came he
had invested 29,000*l*. in the purchase of land alone.
But at this time only the kernel of the subsequent estate
was bought, in the shape of a hundred acres or rather
more, part of which ran along the shores of the Tweed—
"a beautiful river flowing broad and bright over a bed
of milk-white pebbles, unless here and there where it
darkened into a deep pool, overhung as yet only by
birches and alders." There was also a poor farm-house, a
staring barn, and a pond so dirty that it had hitherto given
the name of "Clarty Hole" to the place itself. Scott re-
named the place from the adjoining ford which was just
above the confluence of the Gala with the Tweed. He chose
the name of Abbotsford because the land had formerly all
belonged to the Abbots of Melrose,—the ruin of whose
beautiful abbey was visible from many parts of the little

---

[1] Lockhart's *Life of Scott*, iv. 3.

property. On the other side of the river the old British barrier called "the Catrail" was full in view. As yet the place was not planted,—the only effort made in this direction by its former owner, Dr. Douglas, having been a long narrow stripe of firs, which Scott used to compare to a black hair-comb, and which gave the name of "The Doctor's Redding-Kame" to the stretch of woods of which it is still the central line. Such was the place which he made it the too great delight of the remainder of his life to increase and beautify, by spending on it a good deal more than he had earned, and that too in times when he should have earned a good deal more than he ought to have thought even for a moment of spending. The cottage grew to a mansion, and the mansion to a castle. The farm by the Tweed made him long for a farm by the Cauldshiel's loch, and the farm by the Cauldshiel's loch for Thomas the Rhymer's Glen; and as, at every step in the ladder, his means of buying were really increasing—though they were so cruelly discounted and forestalled by this growing land-hunger,—Scott never realized into what troubles he was carefully running himself.

Of his life at Abbotsford at a later period when his building was greatly enlarged, and his children grown up, we have a brilliant picture from the pen of Mr. Lockhart. And though it does not belong to his first years at Abbotsford, I cannot do better than include it here as conveying probably better than anything I could elsewhere find, the charm of that ideal life which lured Scott on from one project to another in that scheme of castle-building, in relation to which he confused so dangerously the world of dreams with the harder world of wages, capital, interest, and rent.

" I remember saying to William Allan one morning, as the whole party mustered before the porch after breakfast, ' A faithful sketch of what you at this moment see would be more interesting a hundred years hence than the grandest so-called historical picture that you will ever exhibit in Somerset House;' and my friend agreed with me so cordially that I often wondered afterwards he had not attempted to realize the suggestion.   The subject ought, however, to have been treated conjointly by him (or Wilkie) and Edwin Landseer.

" It was a clear, bright September morning, with a sharp-ness in the air that doubled the animating influence of the sunshine, and all was in readiness for a grand coursing match on Newark Hill.   The only guest who had chalked out other sport for himself was the staunchest of anglers, Mr. Rose; but he too was there on his *shelty*, armed with his salmon-rod and landing-net, and attended by his humorous squire, Hinves, and Charlie Purdie, a brother of Tom, in those days the most celebrated fisherman of the district.    This little group of Waltonians, bound for Lord Somerville's preserve, remained lounging about to witness the start of the main cavalcade.   Sir Walter, mounted on Sybil, was marshalling the order of procession with a huge hunting-whip; and among a dozen frolicsome youths and maidens, who seemed disposed to laugh at all discipline, appeared, each on horse-back, each as eager as the youngest sportsman in the troop, Sir Humphry Davy, Dr. Wollaston, and the patriarch of Scottish *belles lettres*, Henry Mackenzie. The Man of Feeling, however, was persuaded with some difficulty to resign his steed for the present to his faithful negro follower, and to join Lady Scott in the sociable, until we should reach the ground of our *battue*.   Laidlaw, on a long-tailed, wiry Highlander, yclept Hoddin Grey, which carried him nimbly and stoutly, although his feet almost touched the ground as he sat, was the adjutant.   But the most picturesque figure was the illustrious inventor of the safety-lamp.   He had come for his favourite sport of angling, and had been practising it successfully with Rose, his travelling-companion, for two or three days preceding this, but he had not pre-pared for coursing fields, and had left Charlie Purdie's

troop for Sir Walter's on a sudden thought; and his
fisherman's costume—a brown hat with flexible brim, surrounded with line upon line, and innumerable fly-hooks,
jack-boots worthy of a Dutch smuggler, and a fustian surtout
dabbled with the blood of salmon,—made a fine contrast with
the smart jackets, white cord breeches, and well-polished
jockey-boots of the less distinguished cavaliers about him.
Dr. Wollaston was in black, and, with his noble, serene
dignity of countenance, might have passed for a sporting
archbishop. Mr. Mackenzie, at this time in the seventy-
sixth year of his age, with a white hat turned up with green,
green spectacles, green jacket, and long brown leather
gaiters buttoned upon his nether anatomy, wore a dog-
whistle round his neck, and had all over the air of as reso-
lute a devotee as the gay captain of Huntly Burn. Tom
Purdie and his subalterns had preceded us by a few hours
with all the greyhounds that could be collected at Abbotsford, Darnick, and Melrose; but the giant Maida had
remained as his master's orderly, and now gambolled about
Sibyl Grey, barking for mere joy, like a spaniel puppy.

" The order of march had been all settled, and the sociable
was just getting under weigh, when *the Lady Anne* broke
from the line, screaming with laughter, and exclaimed,
'Papa! papa! I know you could never think of going without your pet.' Scott looked round, and I rather think there
was a blush as well as a smile upon his face, when he perceived a little black pig frisking about his pony, and evidently a self-elected addition to the party of the day. He
tried to look stern, and cracked his whip at the creature, but
was in a moment obliged to join in the general cheers.
Poor piggy soon found a strap round his neck, and was
dragged into the background. Scott, watching the retreat,
repeated with mock pathos the first verse of an old pastoral
song :—

> " What will I do gin my hoggie die ?
> My joy, my pride, my hoggie !
> My only beast, I had nae mae,
> And wow ! but I was vogie ! "

The cheers were redoubled, and the squadron moved on. This pig had taken, nobody could tell how, a most sentimental attachment to Scott, and was constantly urging its pretension to be admitted a regular member of his *tail*, along with the greyhounds and terriers; but indeed I remember him suffering another summer under the same sort of pertinacity on the part of an affectionate hen. I leave the explanation for philosophers; but such were the facts. I have too much respect for the vulgarly calumniated donkey to name him in the same category of pets with the pig and the hen; but a year or two after this time, my wife used to drive a couple of these animals in a little garden chair, and whenever her father appeared at the door of our cottage, we were sure to see Hannah More and Lady Morgan (as Anne Scott had wickedly christened them) trotting from their pasture to lay their noses over the paling, and, as Washington Irving says of the old white-haired hedger with the Parisian snuff-box, 'to have a pleasant crack wi' the laird.' " [1]

Carlyle, in his criticism on Scott—a criticism which will hardly, I think, stand the test of criticism in its turn, so greatly does he overdo the reaction against the first excessive appreciation of his genius—adds a contribution of his own to this charming idyll, in reference to the natural fascination which Scott seemed to exert over almost all dumb creatures. A little Blenheim cocker, "one of the smallest, beautifullest, and tiniest of lapdogs," with which Carlyle was well acquainted, and which was also one of the shyest of dogs, that would crouch towards his mistress and draw back " with angry timidity " if any one did but look at him admiringly, once met in the street " a tall, singular, busy-looking man," who halted by. The dog ran towards him and began " fawning, frisking, licking at his feet;" and every time he saw Sir Walter

[1] Lockhart's *Life of Scott*, vi. 238—242.

afterwards, in Edinburgh, he repeated his demonstration of delight. Thus discriminating was this fastidious Blenheim cocker even in the busy streets of Edinburgh.

And Scott's attraction for dumb animals was only a lesser form of his attraction for all who were in any way dependent on him, especially his own servants and labourers. The story of his demeanour towards them is one of the most touching ever written. " Sir Walter speaks to every man as if they were blood-relations" was the common *formula* in which this demeanour was described. Take this illustration. There was a little hunchbacked tailor, named William Goodfellow, living on his property (but who at Abbotsford was termed Robin Goodfellow). This tailor was employed to make the curtains for the new library, and had been very proud of his work, but fell ill soon afterwards, and Sir Walter was unremitting in his attention to him. "I can never forget," says Mr. Lockhart, "the evening on which the poor tailor died. When Scott entered the hovel, he found everything silent, and inferred from the looks of the good women in attendance that the patient had fallen asleep, and that they feared his sleep was the final one. He murmured some syllables of kind regret : at the sound of his voice the dying tailor unclosed his eyes, and eagerly and wistfully sat up, clasping his hands with an expression of rapturous gratefulness and devotion that, in the midst of deformity, disease, pain, and wretchedness, was at once beautiful and sublime. He cried with a loud voice, 'The Lord bless and reward you!' and expired with the effort."[1] Still more striking is the account of his relation with Tom Purdie, the wide-

---

[1] Lockhart's *Life of Scott*, vii. 218.

mouthed, under-sized, broad-shouldered, square-made, thin-
flanked woodsman, so well known afterwards by all Scott's
friends as he waited for his master in his green shooting-
jacket, white hat, and drab trousers.    Scott first made
Tom Purdie's acquaintance in his capacity as judge, the
man being brought before him for poaching, at the time
that Scott was living at Ashestiel.    Tom gave so touching
an account of his circumstances—work scarce—wife and
children in want—grouse abundant—and his account of
himself was so fresh and even humorous, that Scott let
him off the penalty, and made him his shepherd.    He
discharged these duties so faithfully that he came to be
his master's forester and factotum, and indeed one of his
best friends, though a little disposed to tyrannize over
Scott in his own fashion.    A visitor describes him as
unpacking a box of new importations for his master "as if
he had been sorting some toys for a restless child."    But
after Sir Walter had lost the bodily strength requisite
for riding, and was too melancholy for ordinary conversation, Tom Purdie's shoulder was his great stay in wandering through his woods, for with him he felt that he
might either speak or be silent at his pleasure.    "What
a blessing there is," Scott wrote in his diary at that time,
"in a fellow like Tom, whom no familiarity can spoil,
whom you may scold and praise and joke with, knowing
the quality of the man is unalterable in his love and
reverence to his master."    After Scott's failure, Mr.
Lockhart writes : " Before I leave this period, I must
note how greatly I admired the manner in which all his
dependents appeared to have met the reverse of his fortunes—a reverse which inferred very considerable altera-
tion in the circumstances of every one of them.  The butler,
instead of being the easy chief of a large establishment,

was now doing half the work of the house at probably half his former wages.   Old Peter, who had been for five and twenty years a dignified coachman, was now plough-man in ordinary, only putting his horses to the carriage upon high and rare occasions; and so on with all the rest that remained of the ancient train.   And all, to my view, seemed happier than they had ever done before."[1]   The illustration of this true confidence between Scott and his servants and labourers might be extended to almost any length.

[1] Lockhart's *Life of Scott*, ix. 170.

# CHAPTER IX.

BEFORE I make mention of Scott's greatest works, his novels, I must say a few words of his relation to the Ballantyne Brothers, who involved him, and were involved by him, in so many troubles, and with whose name the story of his broken fortunes is inextricably bound up. James Ballantyne, the elder brother, was a schoolfellow of Scott's at Kelso, and was the editor and manager of the *Kelso Mail*, an anti-democratic journal, which had a fair circulation. Ballantyne was something of an artist as regarded "type," and Scott got him therefore to print his *Minstrelsy of the Border*, the excellent workmanship of which attracted much attention in London. In 1802, on Scott's suggestion, Ballantyne moved to Edinburgh; and to help him to move, Scott, who was already meditating some investment of his little capital in business other than literary, lent him 500*l*. Between this and 1805, when Scott first became a partner of Ballantyne's in the printing business, he used every exertion to get legal and literary printing offered to James Ballantyne, and, according to Mr. Lockhart, the concern "grew and prospered." At Whitsuntide, 1805, when *The Lay* had been published, but before Scott had the least idea of the prospects of gain which mere literature would open to him, he formally, though secretly, joined Ballantyne as a partner in the printing business. He explains his motives for this step, so far at least as he then recalled them, in a letter written after his misfortunes, in 1826. " It is easy," he said, " no doubt for any friend to blame me for entering into connexion with commercial matters at all. But I wish to know what I could have done better—excluded from the bar, and then from all profits for six years, by my colleague's prolonged life. Literature was not in those days what poor Constable has made it ; and with my little capital I was too glad to make commercially the means of supporting my family. I got but 600*l.* for *The Lay of the Last Minstrel*, and—it was a price that made men's hair stand on end—1000*l.* for *Marmion*. I have been far from suffering by James Ballantyne. I owe it to him to say, that his difficulties, as well as his advantages, are owing to me."

This, though a true, was probably a very imperfect account of Scott's motives. He ceased practising at the bar, I do not doubt, in great degree from a kind of hurt pride at his ill-success, at a time when he felt during every month more and more confidence in his own powers. He believed, with some justice, that he understood some of the secrets of popularity in literature, but he had always, till towards the end of his life, the greatest horror of resting on literature alone as his main resource ; and he was not a man, nor was Lady Scott a woman, to pinch and live narrowly. Were it only for his lavish generosity, that kind of life would have been intolerable to him. Hence, he reflected, that if he could but use his literary instinct to feed some commercial undertaking, managed by a man he could trust, he might gain a considerable percentage on his little capital, without so embarking in commerce

as to oblige him either to give up his status as a sheriff,
or his official duties as a clerk of session, or his literary
undertakings.  In his old schoolfellow, James Ballantyne,
he believed he had found just such an agent as he
wanted, the requisite link between literary genius like
his own, and the world which reads and buys books;
and he thought that, by feeling his way a little, he might
secure, through this partnership, besides the then very
bare rewards of authorship, at least a share in those
more liberal rewards which commercial men managed to
squeeze for themselves out of successful authors.  And,
further, he felt—and this was probably the greatest unconscious attraction for him in this scheme—that with
James Ballantyne for his partner he should be the real
leader and chief, and rather in the position of a patron
and benefactor of his colleague, than of one in any degree
dependent on the generosity or approval of others.  "If
I have a very strong passion in the world," he once wrote
of himself—and the whole story of his life seems to con-
firm it—"it is pride."[1]  In James Ballantyne he had
a faithful, but almost humble friend, with whom he could
deal much as he chose, and fear no wound to his pride.
He had himself helped Ballantyne to a higher line of
business than any hitherto aspired to by him.  It was
his own book which first got the Ballantyne press its
public credit.  And if he could but create a great commercial success upon this foundation, he felt that he should
be fairly entitled to share in the gains, which not merely
his loan of capital, but his foresight and courage had
opened to Ballantyne.

And it is quite possible that Scott might have succeeded—or at all events not seriously failed—if he had

[1] Lockhart's *Life of Scott*, viii. 221.

been content to stick to the printing firm of James Ballantyne and Co., and had not launched also into the bookselling and publishing firm of John Ballantyne and Co.,
or had never begun the wild and dangerous practice of
forestalling his gains, and spending wealth which he had
not earned.  But when by way of feeding the printing
press of James Ballantyne and Co., he started in 1809
the bookselling and publishing firm of John Ballantyne
and Co., using as his agent a man as inferior in sterling
worth to James, as James was inferior in general ability
to himself, he carefully dug a mine under his own feet,
of which we can only say, that nothing except his genius
could have prevented it from exploding long before it
did.   The truth was evidently that James Ballantyne's
respectful homage, and John's humorous appreciation,
all but blinded Scott's eyes to the utter inadequacy of
either of these men, especially the latter, to supply the
deficiencies of his own character for conducting business
of this kind with proper discretion.   James Ballantyne,
who was pompous and indolent, though thoroughly
honest, and not without some intellectual insight, Scott
used to call Aldiborontiphoscophornio.   John, who was
clever but frivolous, dissipated, and tricksy, he termed
Rigdumfunnidos, or his "little Picaroon."   It is clear
from Mr. Lockhart's account of the latter that Scott
not only did not respect, but despised him, though he
cordially liked him, and that he passed over, in judging
him, vices which in a brother or son of his own he would
severely have rebuked.   I believe myself that his liking
for co-operation with both, was greatly founded on his
feeling that they were simply creatures of his, to whom he
could pretty well dictate what he wanted,—colleagues whose
inferiority to himself unconsciously flattered his pride.

He was evidently inclined to resent bitterly the patronage
of publishers. He sent word to Blackwood once with
great hauteur, after some suggestion from that house
had been made to him which appeared to him to interfere
with his independence as an author, that he was one
of " the Black Hussars " of literature, who would not endure that sort of treatment. Constable, who was really
very liberal, hurt his sensitive pride through the *Edinburgh Review*, of which Jeffrey was editor. Thus the
Ballantynes' great deficiency—that neither of them had
any independent capacity for the publishing business, which
would in any way hamper his discretion—though this
is just what commercial partners ought to have had, or
they were not worth their salt,—was, I believe, precisely
what induced this Black Hussar of literature, in spite
of his otherwise considerable sagacity and knowledge of
human nature, to select them for partners.

And yet it is strange that he not only chose them, but
chose the inferior and lighter-headed of the two for far the
most important and difficult of the two businesses. In the
printing concern there was at least this to be said, that
of part of the business—the selection of type and the
superintendence of the executive part,—James Ballantyne was a good judge. He was never apparently a
good man of business, for he kept no strong hand over
the expenditure and accounts, which is the core of success
in every concern. But he understood types ; and his
customers were publishers, a wealthy and judicious class,
who were not likely all to fail together. But to select a
" Rigdumfunnidos,"—a dissipated comic-song singer and
horse-fancier,—for the head of a publishing concern, was
indeed a kind of insanity. It is told of John Ballantyne,
that after the successful negotiation with Constable for

*Rob Roy*, and while "hopping up and down in his glee," he exclaimed, "'Is Rob's gun here, Mr. Scott? Would you object to my trying the old barrel with a *few de joy?*' 'Nay, Mr. Puff,' said Scott, 'it would burst and blow you to the devil before your time.' 'Johnny, my man,' said Constable, 'what the mischief puts drawing at sight into *your* head?' Scott laughed heartily at this innuendo; and then observing that the little man felt somewhat sore, called attention to the notes of a bird in the adjoining shrubbery. 'And by-the-bye,' said he, as they continued listening, ''tis a long time, Johnny, since we have had "The Cobbler of Kelso."' Mr. Puff forthwith jumped up on a mass of stone, and seating himself in the proper attitude of one working with an awl, began a favourite interlude, mimicking a certain son of Crispin, at whose stall Scott and he had often lingered when they were schoolboys, and a blackbird, the only companion of his cell, that used to sing to him while he talked and whistled to it all day long. With this performance Scott was always delighted. Nothing could be richer than the contrast of the bird's wild, sweet notes, some of which he imitated with wonderful skill, and the accompaniment of the cobbler's hoarse, cracked voice, uttering all manner of endearing epithets, which Johnny multiplied and varied in a style worthy of the old women in Rabelais at the birth of Pantagruel." [1] That passage gives precisely the kind of estimation in which John Ballantyne was held both by Scott and Constable. And yet it was to him that Scott entrusted the dangerous and difficult duty of setting up a new publishing house as a rival to the best publishers of the day. No doubt Scott really

---

[1] Lockhart's *Life of Scott*, v. 218.

relied on his own judgment for working the publishing
house.   But except where his own books were concerned,
no judgment could have been worse.   In the first place he
was always wanting to do literary jobs for a friend, and so
advised the publishing of all sorts of unsaleable books, because his friends desired to write them.   In the next place,
he was a genuine historian, and one of the antiquarian
kind himself; he was himself really interested in all sorts
of historical and antiquarian issues,—and very mistakenly
gave the public credit for wishing to know what he himself wished to know.   I should add that Scott's good
nature and kindness of heart not only led him to help on
many books which he knew in himself could never
answer, and some which, as he well knew, would be altogether worthless, but that it greatly biassed his own
intellectual judgment.   Nothing can be plainer than that
he really held his intimate friend, Joanna Baillie, a very
great dramatic poet, a much greater poet than himself, for
instance ; one fit to be even mentioned as following—at a
distance—in the track of Shakespeare.   He supposes
Erskine to exhort him thus :—

> " Or, if to touch such chord be thine,
>     Restore the ancient tragic line,
>     And emulate the notes that rung
>     From the wild harp which silent hung
>     By silver Avon's holy shore,
>     Till twice a hundred years roll'd o'er,—
>     When she, the bold enchantress, came
>     With fearless hand and heart on flame,
>     From the pale willow snatch'd the treasure,
>     And swept it with a kindred measure,
>     Till Avon's swans, while rung the grove
>     With Montfort's hate and Basil's love,
>     Awakening at the inspired strain,
>     Deem'd their own Shakespeare lived again."

Avon's swans must have been Avon's geese, I think, if
they had deemed anything of the kind.  Joanna Baillie's
dramas are " nice," and rather dull ; now and then she
can write a song with the ease and sweetness that suggest
Shakespearian echoes.  But Scott's judgment was obviously
blinded by his just and warm regard for Joanna Baillie
herself.

Of course with such interfering causes to bring unsaleable books to the house—of course I do not mean that
John Ballantyne and Co. published for Joanna Baillie, or that they would have lost by it if they had—the
new firm published all sorts of books which did not sell
at all ; while John Ballantyne himself indulged in a great
many expenses and dissipations, for which John Ballantyne and Co. had to pay.  Nor was it very easy for a
partner who himself drew bills on the future—even
though he were the well-spring of all the paying business
the company had—to be very severe on a fellow-partner
who supplied his pecuniary needs in the same way.
At all events, there is no question that all through 1813
and 1814 Scott was kept in constant suspense and fear of
bankruptcy, by the ill-success of John Ballantyne and
Co., and the utter want of straightforwardness in John
Ballantyne himself as to the bills out, and which had
to be provided against.  It was the publication of *Waverley,* and the consequent opening up of the richest vein
not only in Scott's own genius, but in his popularity with
the public, which alone ended these alarms ; and the
many unsaleable works of John Ballantyne and Co.
were then gradually disposed of to Constable and others,
to their own great loss, as part of the conditions on which
they received a share in the copyright of the wonderful
novels which sold like wildfire.  But though in this way

the publishing business of John Ballantyne and Co.
was saved, and its affairs pretty decently wound up, the
printing firm remained saddled with some of their obligations ; while Constable's business, on which Scott de-
pended for the means with which he was buying his
estate, building his castle, and settling money on his
daughter-in-law, was seriously injured by the purchase of
all this unsaleable stock.

I do not think that any one who looks into the complicated controversy between the representatives of the Ballantynes and Mr. Lockhart, concerning these matters, can
be content with Mr. Lockhart's—no doubt perfectly sincere
—judgment on the case.   It is obvious that amidst these
intricate accounts, he fell into one or two serious blunders
—blunders very unjust to James Ballantyne.  And without
pretending to have myself formed any minute judgment
on the details, I think the following points clear :—
(1.) That James Ballantyne was very severely judged by
Mr. Lockhart, on grounds which were never alleged by
Scott against him at all,—indeed on grounds on which
he was expressly exempted from all blame by Sir Walter.
(2.) That Sir Walter Scott was very severely judged by
the representatives of the Ballantynes, on grounds on
which James Ballantyne himself never brought any charge
against him ; on the contrary, he declared that he had no
charge to bring.   (3.) That both Scott and his partners invited ruin by freely spending gains which they
only expected to earn, and that in this Scott certainly set
an example which he could hardly expect feebler men not
to follow.   On the whole, I think the troubles with the
Ballantyne brothers brought to light not only that eager
gambling spirit in him, which his grandfather indulged
with better success and more moderation when he bought

the hunter with money destined for a flock of sheep, and
then gave up gambling for ever, but a tendency still more
dangerous, and in some respects involving an even greater
moral defect,—I mean a tendency, chiefly due, I think,
to a very deep-seated pride,—to prefer inferior men as
working colleagues in business. And yet it is clear that if
Scott were to dabble in publishing at all, he really needed
the check of men of larger experience, and less literary
turn of mind. The great majority of consumers of popular
literature are not, and indeed will hardly ever be, literary
men ; and that is precisely why a publisher who is not, in
the main, literary,—who looks on authors' MSS. for the
most part with distrust and suspicion, much as a rich man
looks at a begging-letter, or a sober and judicious fish at
an angler's fly,—is so much less likely to run aground
than such a man as Scott. The untried author should be
regarded by a wise publisher as a natural enemy,—an
enemy indeed of a class, rare specimens whereof will
always be his best friends, and who, therefore, should not
be needlessly affronted—but also as one of a class of
whom nineteen out of every twenty will dangle before the
publisher's eyes wiles and hopes and expectations of the
most dangerous and illusory character,—which constitute
indeed the very perils that it is his true function in life
skilfully to evade. The Ballantynes were quite unfit for
this function ; first, they had not the experience requisite
for it ; next, they were altogether too much under Scott's
influence. No wonder that the partnership came to no
good, and left behind it the germs of calamity even more
serious still.

## CHAPTER X.

### THE WAVERLEY NOVELS.

IN the summer of 1814, Scott took up again and completed—almost at a single heat,—a fragment of a Jacobite
story, begun in 1805 and then laid aside. It was published anonymously, and its astonishing success turned
back again the scales of Scott's fortunes, already inclining
ominously towards a catastrophe. This story was *Waverley*. Mr. Carlyle has praised *Waverley* above its fellows.
"On the whole, contrasting *Waverley*, which was carefully written, with most of its followers which were
written extempore, one may regret the extempore method."
This is, however, a very unfortunate judgment. Not one
of the whole series of novels appears to have been written
more completely extempore than the great bulk of *Waverley*, including almost everything that made it either popular
with the million or fascinating to the fastidious; and it
is even likely that this is one of the causes of its excel-
lence.

"The last two volumes," says Scott, in a letter to Mr.
Morritt, "were written in three weeks." And here is
Mr. Lockhart's description of the effect which Scott's in-
cessant toil during the composition, produced on a friend
whose window happened to command the novelist's
study :—

" Happening to pass through Edinburgh in June, 1814, I
dined one day with the gentleman in question (now the
Honourable William Menzies, one of the Supreme Judges at
the Cape of Good Hope), whose residence was then in George
Street, situated very near to, and at right angles with,
North Castle Street.  It was a party of very young persons,
most of them, like Menzies and myself, destined for the
Bar of Scotland, all gay and thoughtless, enjoying the first
flush of manhood, with little remembrance of the yesterday,
or care of the morrow.   When my companion's worthy father
and uncle, after seeing two or three bottles go round, left the
juveniles to themselves, the weather being hot, we adjourned
to a library which had one large window looking northwards.
After carousing here for an hour or more, I observed that a
shade had come over the aspect of my friend, who happened to be placed immediately opposite to myself, and said
something that intimated a fear of his being unwell.  'No,'
said he, 'I shall be well enough presently, if you will only
let me sit where you are, and take my chair; for there is a
confounded hand in sight of me here, which has often
bothered me before, and now it won't let me fill my glass
with a good will.'  I rose to change places with him accordingly, and he pointed out to me this hand, which, like the
writing on Belshazzar's wall, disturbed his hour of hilarity.
'Since we sat down,' he said, 'I have been watching it—
it fascinates my eye—it never stops—page after page is
finished, and thrown on that heap of MS., and still it goes on
unwearied ; and so it will be till candles are brought in, and
God knows how long after that.  It is the same every night
—I can't stand a sight of it when I am not at my books.'
'Some stupid, dogged engrossing clerk, probably,' exclaimed myself, 'or some other giddy youth in our society.'
'No, boys,' said our host; 'I well know what hand it is—
'tis Walter Scott's.' " [1]

If that is not extempore writing, it is difficult to say
what extempore writing is.   But in truth there is no

[1] Lockhart's *Life of Scott*, iv. 171-3.

evidence that any one of the novels was laboured, or even
so much as carefully composed.  Scott's method of composition was always the same; and, when writing an
imaginative work, the rate of progress seems to have
been pretty even, depending much more on the absence of
disturbing engagements, than on any mental irregularity.
The morning was always his brightest time ; but morning
or evening, in country or in town, well or ill, writing
with his own pen or dictating to an amanuensis in the
intervals of screaming-fits due to the torture of cramp in
the stomach, Scott spun away at his imaginative web
almost as evenly as a silkworm spins at its golden cocoon.
Nor can I detect the slightest trace of any difference in
quality between the stories, such as can be reasonably
ascribed to comparative care or haste.  There are differences, and even great differences, of course, ascribable to
the less or greater suitability of the subject chosen to
Scott's genius, but I can find no trace of the sort of
cause to which Mr. Carlyle refers.  Thus, few, I suppose,
would hesitate to say that while *Old Mortality* is very
near, if not quite, the finest of Scott's works, *The
Black Dwarf* is not far from the other end of the scale.
Yet the two were written in immediate succession (*The
Black Dwarf* being the first of the two), and were published together, as the first series of *Tales of my Landlord,* in 1816.  Nor do I think that any competent critic
would find any clear deterioration of quality in the novels
of the later years,—excepting of course the two written
after the stroke of paralysis.  It is true, of course, that
some of the subjects which most powerfully stirred his
imagination were among his earlier themes, and that
he could not effectually use the same subject twice,
though he now and then tried it.  But making allowance

for this consideration, the imaginative power of the novels is as astonishingly *even* as the rate of composition itself. For my own part, I greatly prefer *The Fortunes of Nigel* (which was written in 1822) to *Waverley* which was begun in 1805, and finished in 1814, and though very many better critics would probably decidedly disagree, I do not think that any of them would consider this preference grotesque or purely capricious. Indeed, though *Anne of Geierstein,*—the last composed before Scott's stroke,—would hardly seem to any careful judge the equal of *Waverley*, I do not much doubt that if it had appeared in place of *Waverley*, it would have excited very nearly as much interest and admiration; nor that had *Waverley* appeared in 1829, in place of *Anne of Geierstein*, it would have failed to excite very much more. In these fourteen most effective years of Scott's literary life, during which he wrote twenty-three novels besides shorter tales, the best stories appear to have been on the whole the most rapidly written, probably because they took the strongest hold of the author's imagination.

Till near the close of his career as an author, Scott never avowed his responsibility for any of these series of novels, and even took some pains to mystify the public as to the identity between the author of *Waverley* and the author of *Tales of my Landlord*. The care with which the secret was kept is imputed by Mr. Lockhart in some degree to the habit of mystery which had grown upon Scott during his secret partnership with the Ballantynes; but in this he seems to be confounding two very different phases of Scott's character. No doubt he was, as a professional man, a little ashamed of his commercial speculation, and unwilling to betray it. But he was far from ashamed of his literary enterprise, though it seems

H

that he was at first very anxious lest a comparative
failure, or even a mere moderate success, in a less ambitious sphere than that of poetry, should endanger the
great reputation he had gained as a poet.   That was
apparently the first reason for secrecy.   But, over and
above this, it is clear that the mystery stimulated Scott's
imagination and saved him trouble as well.   He was
obviously more free under the veil—free from the liability
of having to answer for the views of life or history
suggested in his stories ; but besides this, what was of
more importance to him, the slight disguise stimulated his
sense of humour, and gratified the whimsical, boyish
pleasure which he always had in acting an imaginary
character.   He used to talk of himself as a sort of Abon
Hassan—a private man one day, and acting the part of a
monarch the next—with the kind of glee which indicated
a real delight in the change of parts, and I have little
doubt that he threw himself with the more gusto into
characters very different from his own, in consequence of
the pleasure it gave him to conceive his friends hopelessly
misled by this display of traits, with which he supposed
that they could not have credited him even in imagination.
Thus besides relieving him of a host of compliments which
he did not enjoy, and enabling him the better to evade
an ill-bred curiosity, the disguise no doubt was the same
sort of fillip to the fancy which a mask and domino or a
fancy dress are to that of their wearers.   Even in a disguise
a man cannot cease to be himself ; but he can get rid of
his improperly " imputed " righteousness—often the
greatest burden he has to bear—and of all the expectations
formed on the strength, as Mr. Clough says,—

> " Of having been what one has been,
> What one thinks one is, or thinks that others suppose one."

To some men the freedom of this disguise is a real danger and temptation. It never could have been so to Scott, who was in the main one of the simplest as well as the boldest and proudest of men. And as most men perhaps would admit that a good deal of even the best part of their nature is rather suppressed than expressed by the name by which they are known in the world, Scott must have felt this in a far higher degree, and probably regarded the manifold characters under which he was known to society, as representing him in some respects more justly than any individual name could have done. His mind ranged hither and thither over a wide field—far beyond that of his actual experience,—and probably ranged over it all the more easily for not being absolutely tethered to a single class of associations by any public confession of his authorship. After all, when it became universally known that Scott was the only author of all these tales, it may be doubted whether the public thought as adequately of the imaginative efforts which had created them, as they did while they remained in some doubt whether there was a multiplicity of agencies at work, or only one. The uncertainty helped them to realize the many lives which were really led by the author of all these tales, more completely than any confession of the individual authorship could have done. The shrinking of activity in public curiosity and wonder which follows the final determination of such ambiguities, is very apt to result rather in a dwindling of the imaginative effort to enter into the genius which gave rise to them, than in an increase of respect for so manifold a creative power.

When Scott wrote, such fertility as his in the production of novels was regarded with amazement approaching to absolute incredulity. Yet he was in this respect only the advanced-guard of a not inconsiderable class of men and women who have a special gift for pouring out story after story, containing a great variety of figures, while retaining a certain even level of merit. There is more than one novelist of the present day who has far surpassed Scott in the number of his tales, and one at least of very high repute, who has, I believe, produced more even within the same time. But though to our larger experience, Scott's achievement, in respect of mere fertility, is by no means the miracle which it once seemed, I do not think one of his successors can compare with him for a moment in the ease and truth with which he painted, not merely the life of his own time and country—seldom indeed that of precisely his own time—but that of days long past, and often too of scenes far distant. The most powerful of all his stories, *Old Mortality*, was the story of a period more than a century and a quarter before he wrote; and others,—which though inferior to this in force, are nevertheless, when compared with the so-called historical romances of any other English writer, what sunlight is to moonlight, if you can say as much for the latter as to admit even that comparison,—go back to the period of the Tudors, that is, two centuries and a half. *Quentin Durward*, which is all but amongst the best, runs back farther still, far into the previous century, while *Ivanhoe* and *The Talisman*, though not among the greatest of Scott's works, carry us back more than five hundred years. The new class of extempore novel writers, though more considerable than, sixty years ago, any one could have expected ever to see it, is still limited, and on any high level of merit will probably always be limited, to the delineation of the times of which the narrator has personal experience. Scott seemed to have had something very

like personal experience of a few centuries at least, judging
by the ease and freshness with which he poured out his
stories of these centuries, and though no one can pretend
that even he could describe the period of the Tudors as
Miss Austen described the country parsons and squires of
George the Third's reign, or as Mr. Trollope describes the
politicians and hunting-men of Queen Victoria's, it is nevertheless the evidence of a greater imagination to make us live
so familiarly as Scott does amidst the political and religious
controversies of two or three centuries' duration, to be the
actual witnesses, as it were, of Margaret of Anjou's throes
of vain ambition, and Mary Stuart's fascinating remorse,
and Elizabeth's domineering and jealous balancings of
noble against noble, of James the First's shrewd pedantries,
and the Regent Murray's large forethought, of the politic
craft of Argyle, the courtly ruthlessness of Claverhouse,
and the high-bred clemency of Monmouth, than to reflect
in countless modifications the freaks, figures, and fashions
of our own time.

The most striking feature of Scott's romances is that,
for the most part, they are pivoted on public rather than
mere private interests and passions. With but few excep-
tions—(*The Antiquary, St. Ronan's Well,* and *Guy Mannering* are the most important)—Scott's novels give us an
imaginative view, not of mere individuals, but of individuals as they are affected by the public strifes and social
divisions of the age. And this it is which gives his books
so large an interest for old and young, soldiers and statesmen, the world of society and the recluse, alike. You can
hardly read any novel of Scott's and not become better
aware what public life and political issues mean. And
yet there is no artificiality, no elaborate attitudinizing
before the antique mirrors of the past, like Bulwer's, no

dressing out of clothes-horses like G. P. R. James. The
boldness and freshness of the present are carried back into
the past, and you see Papists and Puritans, Cavaliers and
Roundheads, Jews, Jacobites, and freebooters, preachers,
schoolmasters, mercenary soldiers, gipsies, and beggars, all
living the sort of life which the reader feels that in their
circumstances and under the same conditions of time and
place and parentage, he might have lived too. Indeed,
no man can read Scott without being more of a public
man, whereas the ordinary novel tends to make its readers
rather less of one than before.

Next, though most of these stories are rightly called
romances, no one can avoid observing that they give that
side of life which is unromantic, quite as vigorously as the
romantic side. This was not true of Scott's poems, which
only expressed one-half of his nature, and were almost pure
romances. But in the novels the business of life is even
better portrayed than its sentiments. Mr. Bagehot, one of
the ablest of Scott's critics, has pointed out this admirably
in his essay on *The Waverley Novels.* " Many historical
novelists," he says, " especialy those who with care and
pains have read up the detail, are often evidently in
a strait how to pass from their history to their sentiment.
The fancy of Sir Walter could not help connecting the
two. If he had given us the English side of the race to
Derby, *he would have described the Bank of England
paying in sixpences, and also the loves of the cashier.*"
No one who knows the novels well can question this.
Fergus MacIvor's ways and means, his careful arrangements for receiving subsidies in black mail, are as carefully recorded as his lavish highland hospitalities; and
when he sends his silver cup to the Gaelic bard who
chaunts his greatness, the faithful historian does not for-

get to let us know that the cup is his last, and that he is
hard-pressed for the generosities of the future.  So too
the habitual thievishness of the highlanders is pressed
upon us quite as vividly as their gallantry and superstitions.  And so careful is Sir Walter to paint the petty
pedantries of the Scotch traditional conservatism, that he
will not spare even Charles Edward—of whom he draws
so graceful a picture—the humiliation of submitting to
old Bradwardine's "solemn act of homage," but makes him
go through the absurd ceremony of placing his foot on a
cushion to have its brogue unlatched by the dry old
enthusiast of heraldic lore.  Indeed it was because Scott
so much enjoyed the contrast between the high sentiment
of life and its dry and often absurd detail, that his imagination found so much freer a vent in the historical
romance, than it ever found in the romantic poem.
Yet he clearly needed the romantic excitement of picturesque scenes and historical interests, too.  I do not
think he would ever have gained any brilliant success in
the narrower region of the domestic novel.  He said himself, in expressing his admiration of Miss Austen, "The big
bow-wow strain I can do myself, like any now going, but
the exquisite touch which renders ordinary commonplace
things and characters interesting, from the truth of the
description and the sentiment, is denied to me."  Indeed
he tried it to some extent in *St. Ronan's Well*, and so far
as he tried it, I think he failed.  Scott needed a certain
largeness of type, a strongly-marked class-life, and, where
it was possible, a free, out-of-doors life, for his delinea-
tions.  No one could paint beggars and gipsies, and wandering fiddlers, and mercenary soldiers, and peasants and
farmers and lawyers, and magistrates, and preachers, and
courtiers, and statesmen, and best of all perhaps queens

and kings, with anything like his ability.   But when it
came to describing the small differences of manner, differences not due to external habits, so much as to internal
sentiment or education, or mere domestic circumstance,
he was beyond his proper field.   In the sketch of the St.
Ronan's Spa and the company at the *table-d'hôte*, he is
of course somewhere near the mark,—he was too able a
man to fall far short of success in anything he really gave
to the world; but it is not interesting.   Miss Austen
would have made Lady Penelope Penfeather a hundred
times as amusing.   We turn to Meg Dods and Touch-
wood, and Cargill, and Captain Jekyl, and Sir Bingo
Binks, and to Clara Mowbray,—i. e. to the lives really
moulded by large and specific causes, for enjoyment, and
leave the small gossip of the company at the Wells as,
relatively at least, a failure.   And it is well for all the world
that it was so.   The domestic novel, when really of the
highest kind, is no doubt a perfect work of art, and an
unfailing source of amusement; but it has nothing of the
tonic influence, the large instructiveness, the stimulating
intellectual air, of Scott's historic tales.   Even when Scott
is farthest from reality—as in *Ivanhoe* or *The Monastery*—he makes you open your eyes to all sorts of historical conditions to which you would otherwise be blind.
The domestic novel, even when its art is perfect, gives
little but pleasure at the best; at the worst it is simply
scandal idealized.

Scott often confessed his contempt for his own heroes.
He said of Edward Waverley, for instance, that he
was "a sneaking piece of imbecility," and that "if he
had married Flora, she would have set him up upon the
chimney-piece as Count Borowlaski's wife used to do
with him.   I am a bad hand at depicting a hero, pro-

perly so called, and have an unfortunate propensity for
the dubious characters of borderers, buccaneers, highland
robbers, and all others of a Robin-Hood description." [1]   In
another letter he says, " My rogue always, in despite of
me, turns out my hero." [2]   And it seems very likely that
in most of the situations Scott describes so well, his own
course would have been that of his wilder impulses,
and not that of his reason.   Assuredly he would never
have stopped hesitating on the line between opposite
courses as his Waverleys, his Mortons, his Osbaldistones
do.   Whenever he was really involved in a party strife,
he flung prudence and impartiality to the winds, and
went in like the hearty partisan which his strong impulses made of him.   But granting this, I do not agree
with his condemnation of all his own colourless heroes.
However much they differed in nature from Scott himself,
the even balance of their reason against their sympathies
is certainly well conceived, is in itself natural, and is an
admirable expedient for effecting that which was probably its real use to Scott,—the affording an opportunity
for the delineation of all the pros and cons of the case, so
that the characters on both sides of the struggle should
be properly understood.   Scott's imagination was clearly
far wider—was far more permeated with the fixed air of
sound judgment—than his practical impulses.   He needed
a machinery for displaying his insight into both sides of a
public quarrel, and his colourless heroes gave him the
instrument he needed.   Both in Morton's case (in *Old
Mortality*), and in Waverley's, the hesitation is certainly
well described.   Indeed in relation to the controversy
between Covenanters and Royalists, while his political

[1] Lockhart's *Life of Scott*, iv. 175-6.
[2] Lockhart's *Life of Scott*, iv. 46.

and martial prepossessions went with Claverhouse, his
reason and educated moral feeling certainly were clearly
identified with Morton.

It is, however, obviously true that Scott's heroes are
mostly created for the sake of the facility they give in de-
lineating the other characters, and not the other characters
for the sake of the heroes. They are the imaginative
neutral ground, as it were, on which opposing influences
are brought to play; and what Scott best loved to paint
was those who, whether by nature, by inheritance, or by
choice, had become unique and characteristic types of
one-sided feeling, not those who were merely in process of
growth, and had not ranged themselves at all. Mr.
Carlyle, who, as I have said before, places Scott's romances
far below their real level, maintains that these great
types of his are drawn from the outside, and not made
actually to live. "His Bailie Jarvies, Dinmonts, Dal-
gettys (for their name is legion), do look and talk like
what they give themselves out for; they are, if not
*created* and made poetically alive, yet deceptively *enacted*
as a good player might do them. What more is wanted,
then? For the reader lying on a sofa, nothing more; yet
for another sort of reader much. It were a long chapter to
unfold the difference in drawing a character between a
Scott and a Shakespeare or Goethe. Yet it is a difference
literally immense; they are of a different species; the
value of the one is not to be counted in the coin of the
other. We might say in a short word, which covers a long
matter, that your Shakespeare fashions his characters from
the heart outwards; your Scott fashions them from the
skin inwards, never getting near the heart of them. The
one set become living men and women; the other amount
to little more than mechanical cases, deceptively painted

automatons."[1]　And then he goes on to contrast Fenella in
*Peveril of the Peak* with Goethe's Mignon.　Mr. Carlyle could hardly have chosen a less fair comparison.　If
Goethe is to be judged by his women, let Scott be judged
by his men.　So judged, I think Scott will, as a painter
of character—of course, I am not now speaking of him as a
poet,—come out far above Goethe.　Excepting the hero
of his first drama (Götz of the iron hand), which by the
way was so much in Scott's line that his first essay in
poetry was to translate it—not very well—I doubt if
Goethe was ever successful with his pictures of men.
*Wilhelm Meister* is, as Niebuhr truly said, "a ména-
gerie of tame animals."　Doubtless Goethe's women—certainly his women of culture—are more truly and inwardly
conceived and created than Scott's.　Except Jeanie
Deans and Madge Wildfire, and perhaps Lucy Ashton,
Scott's women are apt to be uninteresting, either pink and
white toys, or hardish women of the world.　But then no
one can compare the men of the two writers, and not see
Scott's vast pre-eminence on that side.

I think the deficiency of his pictures of women, odd as
it seems to say so, should be greatly attributed to his natural
chivalry.　His conception of women of his own or a higher
class was always too romantic.　He hardly ventured, as it
were, in his tenderness for them, to look deeply into their
little weaknesses and intricacies of character.　With women
of an inferior class, he had not this feeling.　Nothing
can be more perfect than the manner in which he blends
the dairy-woman and woman of business in Jeanie Deans,
with the lover and the sister.　But once make a woman
beautiful, or in any way an object of homage to him, and

---

[1] Carlyle's *Miscellaneous Essays*, iv. 174-5.

Scott bowed so low before the image of her, that he could
not go deep into her heart.  He could no more have analysed such a woman, as Thackeray analyzed Lady Castle-
wood, or Amèlia, or Becky, or as George Eliot analysed
Rosamond Vincy, than he could have vivisected Camp or
Maida.  To some extent, therefore, Scott's pictures of women
remain something in the style of the miniatures of the
last age—bright and beautiful beings without any special
character in them.  He was dazzled by a fair heroine.  He
could not take them up into his imagination as real beings
as he did men.  But then how living are his men, whether
coarse or noble !  What a picture, for instance, is that in
*A Legend of Montrose* of the conceited, pragmatic, but
prompt and dauntless soldier of fortune, rejecting Argyle's
attempts to tamper with him, in the dungeon at Inverary,
suddenly throwing himself on the disguised Duke so soon
as he detects him by his voice, and wresting from him the
means of his own liberation !  Who could read that scene
and say for a moment that Dalgetty is painted "from the
skin inwards"?  It was just Scott himself breathing his own
life through the habits of a good specimen of the mercenary
soldier—realizing where the spirit of hire would end, and
the sense of honour would begin—and preferring, even in a
dungeon, the audacious policy of a sudden attack to that
of crafty negotiation.  What a picture (and a very different
one) again is that in *Redgauntlet* of Peter Peebles, the
mad litigant, with face emaciated by poverty and anxiety,
and rendered wild by "an insane lightness about the eyes,"
dashing into the English magistrate's court for a warrant
against his fugitive counsel.  Or, to take a third instance,
as different as possible from either, how powerfully conceived is the situation in *Old Mortality*, where Balfour of
Burley, in his fanatic fury at the defeat of his plan for a

new rebellion, pushes the oak-tree, which connects his
wild retreat with the outer world, into the stream, and
tries to slay Morton for opposing him.   In such scenes
and a hundred others—for these are mere random examples
—Scott undoubtedly painted his masculine figures from as
deep and inward a conception of the character of the
situation as Goethe ever attained, even in drawing Mignon,
or Klärchen, or Gretchen.   The distinction has no real
existence.   Goethe's pictures of women were no doubt the
intuitions of genius ; and so are Scott's of men—and here
and there of his women too.   Professional women he can
always paint with power.   Meg Dods, the innkeeper, Meg
Merrilies, the gipsy, Mause Headrigg, the Covenanter,
Elspeth, the old fishwife in *The Antiquary*, and the old
crones employed to nurse and watch, and lay out the
corpse, in *The Bride of Lammermoor*, are all in their way
impressive figures.

And even in relation to women of a rank more fascinating to Scott, and whose inner character was perhaps on
that account, less familiar to his imagination, grant him but
a few hints from history, and he draws a picture which,
for vividness and brilliancy, may almost compare with
Shakespeare's own studies in English history.   Had
Shakespeare painted the scene in *The Abbot*, in which
Mary Stuart commands one of her Mary's in waiting to
tell her at what bridal she last danced, and Mary Fleming
blurts out the reference to the marriage of Sebastian at
Holyrood, would any one hesitate to regard it as a stroke
of genius worthy of the great dramatist?   This picture
of the Queen's mind suddenly thrown off its balance, and
betraying, in the agony of the moment, the fear and
remorse which every association with Darnley conjured
up, is painted "from the heart outwards," not "from the

skin inwards," if ever there were such a painting in the
world.    Scott hardly ever failed in painting kings or
peasants, queens or peasant-women.    There was something
in the well-marked type of both to catch his imagination, which can always hit off the grander features of
royalty, and the homelier features of laborious humility.
Is there any sketch traced in lines of more sweeping grandeur and more impressive force than the following of Mary
Stuart's lucid interval of remorse—lucid compared with her
ordinary mood, though it was of a remorse that was almost
delirious—which breaks in upon her hour of fascinating
condescension ?—

  " ' Are they not a lovely couple, my Fleming ? and is it not
heart-rending to think that I must be their ruin ? '
  " ' Not so,' said Roland Græme, ' it is we, gracious sovereign, who will be your deliverers.'   ' *Ex oribus parvu-
lorum !* ' said the queen, looking upward ; ' if it is by the
mouth of these children that heaven calls me to resume the
stately thoughts which become my birth and my rights, thou
wilt grant them thy protection, and to me the power of
rewarding their zeal.'   Then turning to Fleming, she in-
stantly added, ' Thou knowest, my friend, whether to make
those who have served me happy, was not ever Mary's
favourite pastime.   When I have been rebuked by the stern
preachers of the Calvinistic heresy—when I have seen the
fierce countenances of my nobles averted from me, has it
not been because I mixed in the harmless pleasures of the
young and gay, and rather for the sake of their happiness
than my own, have mingled in the masque, the song or
the dance, with the youth of my household ?   Well, I repent
not of it—though Knox termed it sin, and Morton degrada-
tion—I was happy because I saw happiness around me :
and woe betide the wretched jealousy that can extract guilt
out of the overflowings of an unguarded gaiety !—Fleming,
if we are restored to our throne, shall we not have one
blithesome day at a blithesome bridal, of which we must
now name neither the bride nor the bridegroom ?   But that

bridegroom shall have the barony of Blairgowrie, a fair
gift even for a queen to give, and that bride's chaplet shall
be twined with the fairest pearls that ever were found in the
depths of Lochlomond; and thou thyself, Mary Fleming,
the best dresser of tires that ever busked the tresses of a
queen, and who would scorn to touch those of any woman
of lower rank—thou thyself shalt for my love twine them
into the bride's tresses.—Look, my Fleming, suppose then
such clustered locks as these of our Catherine, they would
not put shame upon thy skill.' So saying she passed her
hand fondly over the head of her youthful favourite, while
her more aged attendant replied despondently, 'Alas,
madam, your thoughts stray far from home.' 'They do,
my Fleming,' said the queen, 'but is it well or kind in
you to call them back?—God knows they have kept the
perch this night but too closely.—Come, I will recall the
gay vision, were it but to punish them. Yes, at that
blithesome bridal, Mary herself shall forget the weight of
sorrows, and the toil of state, and herself once more lead a
measure.—At whose wedding was it that we last danced,
my Fleming? I think care has troubled my memory—yet
something of it I should remember, canst thou not aid me?
I know thou canst.' 'Alas, madam,' replied the lady.
'What,' said Mary, 'wilt thou not help us so far? this is
a peevish adherence to thine own graver opinion which holds
our talk as folly. But thou art court-bred and wilt well
understand me when I say the queen *commands* Lady
Fleming to tell her when she led the last *branle*.' With a
face deadly pale and a mien as if she were about to sink
into the earth, the court-bred dame, no longer daring to
refuse obedience, faltered out, 'Gracious lady—if my
marriage of Sebastian.' The unhappy queen, who had
hitherto listened with a melancholy smile, provoked by the
reluctance with which the Lady Fleming brought out her
story, at this ill-fated word interrupted her with a shriek
so wild and loud that the vaulted apartment rang, and
both Roland and Catherine sprung to their feet in the
utmost terror and alarm. Meantime, Mary seemed, by the

train of horrible ideas thus suddenly excited, surprised not
only beyond self-command, but for the moment beyond the
verge of reason. ' Traitress,' she said to the Lady Fleming,
'thou wouldst slay thy sovereign. Call my French guards—
*à moi! à moi! mes Français!*—I am beset with traitors in
mine own palace—they have murdered my husband—
Rescue! Rescue! for the Queen of Scotland!' She started
up from her chair—her features late so exquisitely lovely
in their paleness, now inflamed with the fury of frenzy, and
resembling those of a Bellona. ' We will take the field our-
self,' she said; ' warn the city—warn Lothian and Fife—
saddle our Spanish barb, and bid French Paris see our
petronel be charged. Better to die at the head of our brave
Scotsmen, like our grandfather at Flodden, than of a
broken heart like our ill-starred father.' ' Be patient—be
composed, dearest sovereign,' said Catherine; and then
addressing Lady Fleming angrily, she added, ' How could
you say aught that reminded her of her husband?' The
word reached the ear of the unhappy princess who caught
it up, speaking with great rapidity, ' Husband!—what
husband? Not his most Christian Majesty—he is ill at
ease—he cannot mount on horseback—not him of the
Lennox—but it was the Duke of Orkney thou wouldst say?'
' For God's love, madam, be patient!' said the Lady
Fleming. But the queen's excited imagination could by no
entreaty be diverted from its course. ' Bid him come hither
to our aid,' she said, ' and bring with him his lambs, as he
calls them—Bowton, Hay of Talla, Black Ormiston and
his kinsman Hob—Fie, how swart they are, and how they
smell of sulphur! What! closeted with Morton? Nay, if
the Douglas and the Hepburn hatch the complot together,
the bird when it breaks the shell will scare Scotland, will
it not, my Fleming?' ' She grows wilder and wilder,' said
Fleming. ' We have too many hearers for these strange
words.' ' Roland,' said Catherine, ' in the name of God
begone!—you cannot aid us here—leave us to deal with her
alone—away—away!' "

And equally fine is the scene in *Kenilworth* in which

Elizabeth undertakes the reconciliation of the haughty
rivals, Sussex and Leicester, unaware that in the course
of the audience she herself will have to bear a great strain
on her self-command, both in her feelings as a queen and
her feelings as a lover.  Her grand rebukes to both, her
ill-concealed preference for Leicester, her whispered ridi-
cule of Sussex, the impulses of tenderness which she
stifles, the flashes of resentment to which she gives way,
the triumph of policy over private feeling, her imperious
impatience when she is baffled, her jealousy as she grows
suspicious of a personal rival, her gratified pride and
vanity when the suspicion is exchanged for the clear evidence, as she supposes, of Leicester's love, and her peremptory conclusion of the audience, bring before the mind a
series of pictures far more vivid and impressive than
the greatest of historical painters could fix on canvas,
even at the cost of the labour of years.  Even more
brilliant, though not so sustained and difficult an effort
of genius, is the later scene in the same story, in which
Elizabeth drags the unhappy Countess of Leicester from
her concealment in one of the grottoes of Kenilworth
Castle, and strides off with her, in a fit of vindictive
humiliation and Amazonian fury, to confront her with
her husband.  But this last scene no doubt is more in
Scott's way.  He can always paint women in their more
masculine moods.  Where he frequently fails is in the
attempt to indicate the finer shades of women's nature.
In Amy Robsart herself, for example, he is by no means
generally successful, though in an early scene her childish
delight in the various orders and decorations of her
husband is painted with much freshness and delicacy.
But wherever, as in the case of queens, Scott can get a
telling hint from actual history, he can always so use it

I

as to make history itself seem dim to the equivalent for it which he gives us.

And yet, as every one knows, Scott was excessively free in his manipulations of history for the purposes of romance. In *Kenilworth* he represents Shakespeare's plays as already in the mouths of courtiers and statesmen, though he lays the scene in the eighteenth year of Elizabeth, when Shakespeare was hardly old enough to rob an orchard. In *Woodstock*, on the contrary, he insists, if you compare Sir Henry Lee's dates with the facts, that Shakespeare died twenty years at least before he actually died. The historical basis, again, of *Woodstock* and of *Redgauntlet* is thoroughly untrustworthy, and about all the minuter details of history,—unless so far as they were characteristic of the age,—I do not suppose that Scott in his romances ever troubled himself at all. And yet few historians—not even Scott himself when he exchanged romance for history—ever drew the great figures of history with so powerful a hand. In writing history and biography Scott has little or no advantage over very inferior men. His pictures of Swift, of Dryden, of Napoleon, are in no way very vivid. It is only where he is working from the pure imagination,—though imagination stirred by historic study,—that he paints a picture which follows us about, as if with living eyes, instead of creating for us a mere series of lines and colours. Indeed, whether Scott draws truly or falsely, he draws with such genius that his pictures of Richard and Saladin, of Louis XI. and Charles the Bold,' of Margaret of Anjou and René of Provence, of Mary Stuart and Elizabeth Tudor, of Sussex and of Leicester, of James and Charles and Buckingham, of the two Dukes of Argyle—the Argyle of the time of the revolution, and the Argyle of George II.,—

of Queen Caroline, of Claverhouse, and Monmouth,
and of Rob Roy, will live in English literature beside
Shakespeare's pictures—probably less faithful if more
imaginative—of John and Richard and the later Henries,
and all the great figures by whom they were surrounded.
No historical portrait that we possess will take prece-
dence—as a mere portrait—of Scott's brilliant study
of James I. in *The Fortunes of Nigel.* Take this illustration for instance, where George Heriot the goldsmith
(Jingling Geordie, as the king familiarly calls him) has
just been speaking of Lord Huntinglen, as " a man of the
old rough world that will drink and swear :"—

" ' O Geordie!' exclaimed the king, ' these are auld-warld
frailties, of whilk we dare not pronounce even ourselves
absolutely free.  But the warld grows worse from day to day,
Geordie.  The juveniles of this age may weel say with the
poet,—

> " Ætas parentum pejor avis tulit
> Nos nequiores—"

This Dalgarno does not drink so much, aye or swear so much,
as his father, but he wenches, Geordie, and he breaks his
word and oath baith.  As to what ye say of the leddy and
the ministers, we are all fallible creatures, Geordie, priests
and kings as weel as others; and wha kens but what that
may account for the difference between this Dalgarno and
his father ?  The earl is the vera soul of honour, and cares
nae mair for warld's gear than a noble hound for the quest
of a foulmart; but as for his son, he was like to brazen us
all out—ourselves, Steenie, Baby Charles, and our Council,
till he heard of the tocher, and then by my kingly crown he
lap like a cock at a grossart !  These are discrepancies be-
twixt parent and son not to  be accounted for naturally,
according to Baptista Porta, Michael Scott *de secretis*, and
others.  Ah, Jingling Geordie, if your clouting the caldron,
and jingling on pots, pans, and veshels of all manner of

metal, hadna jingled a' your grammar out of your head, I
could have touched on that matter to you at mair length.'
. . . . Heriot inquired whether Lord Dalgarno had consented
to do the Lady Hermione justice. 'Troth, man, I have
small doubt that he will,' quoth the king, 'I gave him the
schedule of her worldly substance, which you delivered to us
in the council, and we allowed him half an hour to chew
the cud upon that. It is rare reading for bringing him to
reason. I left Baby Charles and Steenie laying his duty
before him, and if he can resist doing what *they* desire
him, why I wish he would teach *me* the gate of it.
O Geordie, Jingling Geordie, it was grand to hear Baby
Charles laying down the guilt of dissimulation, and Steenie
lecturing on the turpitude of incontinence.' 'I am afraid,'
said George Heriot, more hastily than prudently, 'I might
have thought of the old proverb of Satan reproving
sin.' 'Deil hae our saul, neighbour,' said the king, redden-
ing, 'but ye are not blate! I gie ye licence to speak freely,
and by our saul, ye do not let the privilege become lost, *non
utendo*—it will suffer no negative prescription in your
hands. Is it fit, think ye, that Baby Charles should let
his thoughts be publicly seen? No, no, princes' thoughts
are *arcana imperii : qui nescit dissimulare, nescit regnare.*
Every liege subject is bound to speak the whole truth to the
king, but there is nae reciprocity of obligation—and for
Steenie having been whiles a dike-louper at a time, is it
for you, who are his goldsmith, and to whom, I doubt, he
awes an uncomatable sum, to cast that up to him?"

Assuredly there is no undue favouring of Stuarts in
such a picture as that.

Scott's humour is, I think, of very different qualities in
relation to different subjects. Certainly he was at times
capable of considerable heaviness of hand,—of the Scotch
"wut" which has been so irreverently treated by
English critics. His rather elaborate jocular introductions,
under the name of Jedediah Cleishbotham, are clearly

laborious at times.   And even his own letters to his
daughter-in-law, which Mr. Lockhart seems to regard as
models of tender playfulness and pleasantry, seem to me
decidedly elephantine.   Not unfrequently, too, his stereo-
typed jokes weary.   Dalgetty bores you almost as much as
he would do in real life,—which is a great fault in art.   Bradwardine becomes a nuisance, and as for Sir Piercie Shafton,
he is beyond endurance.   Like some other Scotchmen of
genius, Scott twanged away at any effective chord till it
more than lost its expressiveness.   But in dry humour,
and in that higher humour which skilfully blends the
ludicrous and the pathetic, so that it is hardly possible to
separate between smiles and tears, Scott is a master.   His
canny innkeeper, who, having sent away all the pease-
meal to the camp of the Covenanters, and all the oatmeal
(with deep professions of duty) to the castle and its
cavaliers, in compliance with the requisitions sent to
him on each side, admits with a sigh to his daughter
that "they maun gar wheat flour serve themsels for a
blink,"—his firm of solicitors, Greenhorn and Grinder-
son, whose senior partner writes respectfully to clients in
prosperity, and whose junior partner writes familiarly to
those in adversity,—his arbitrary nabob who asks how the
devil any one should be able to mix spices so well "as
one who has been where they grow;"—his little ragamuffin
who indignantly denies that he has broken his promise
not to gamble away his sixpences at pitch-and-toss because
he has gambled them away at " neevie-neevie-nick-nack,"—
and similar figures abound in his tales,—are all creations
which make one laugh inwardly as we read.   But he has
a much higher humour still, that inimitable power of
shading off ignorance into knowledge and simplicity into
wisdom, which makes his picture of Jeanie Deans, for

instance, so humorous as well as so affecting. When
Jeanie reunites her father to her husband by reminding the
former how it would sometimes happen that " twa precious
saints might pu' sundrywise like twa cows riving at the
same hayband," she gives us an admirable instance of
Scott's higher humour. Or take Jeanie Deans's letter to
her father communicating to him the pardon of his
daughter and her own interview with the Queen :—

"DEAREST AND TRULY HONOURED FATHER.—This comes
with my duty to inform you, that it has pleased God to
redeem that captivitie of my poor sister, in respect the
Queen's blessed Majesty, for whom we are ever bound to
pray, hath redeemed her soul from the slayer, granting the
ransom of her, whilk is ane pardon or reprieve. And I spoke
with the Queen face to face, and yet live ; for she is not
muckle differing from other grand leddies, saving that she
has a stately presence, and een like a blue huntin' hawk's,
whilk gaed throu' and throu' me like a Highland durk—And
all this good was, alway under the Great Giver, to whom all
are but instruments, wrought for us by the Duk of Argile,
wha is ane native true-hearted Scotsman, and not pridefu',
like other folk we ken of—and likewise skeely enow in bestial,
whereof he has promised to gie me twa Devonshire kye, of
which he is enamoured, although I do still haud by the real
hawkit Airshire breed—and I have promised him a cheese ;
and I wad wuss ye, if Gowans, the brockit cow, has a quey,
that she suld suck her fill of milk, as I am given to understand he has none of that breed, and is not scornfu' but will
take a thing frae a puir body, that it may lighten their heart
of the loading of debt that they awe him. Also his honour
the Duke will accept ane of our Dunlop cheeses, and it sall
be my faut if a better was ever yearned in Lowden."—[Here
follow some observations respecting the breed of cattle, and
the produce of the dairy, which it is our intention to forward
to the Board of Agriculture.]—" Nevertheless, these are but
matters of the after-harvest, in respect of the great good
which Providence hath gifted us with—and, in especial, poor

Effie's life. And oh, my dear father, since it hath pleased God to be merciful to her, let her not want your free pardon, whilk will make her meet to be ane vessel of grace, and also a comfort to your ain graie hairs. Dear Father, will ye let the Laird ken that we have had friends strangely raised up to us, and that the talent whilk he lent me will be thankfully repaid. I hae some of it to the fore; and the rest of it is not knotted up in ane purse or napkin, but in ane wee bit paper, as is the fashion heir, whilk I am assured is gude for the siller. And, dear father, through Mr. Butler's means I hae gude friendship with the Duke, for there had been kind-ness between their forbears in the auld troublesome time byepast. And Mrs. Glass has been kind like my very mother. She has a braw house here, and lives bien and warm, wi' twa servant lasses, and a man and a callant in the shop. And she is to send you doun a pound of her hie-dried, and some other tobaka, and we maun think of some propine for her, since her kindness hath been great. And the Duk is to send the pardon doun by an express mes-senger, in respect that I canna travel sae fast; and I am to come doun wi' twa of his Honour's servants—that is, John Archibald, a decent elderly gentleman, that says he has seen you lang syne, when ye were buying beasts in the west frae the Laird of Aughtermuggitie—but maybe ye winna mind him—ony way, he's a civil man—and Mrs. Dolly Dutton, that is to be dairy-maid at Inverara: and they bring me on as far as Glasgo', whilk will make it nae pinch to win hame, whilk I desire of all things. May the Giver of all good things keep ye in your outgauns and incomings, whereof devoutly prayeth your loving dauter,

"JEAN DEANS."

This contains an example of Scott's rather heavy jocu-larity as well as giving us a fine illustration of his highest and deepest and sunniest humour. Coming where it does, the joke inserted about the Board of Agriculture is rather like the gambol of a rhinoceros trying to imitate the curvettings of a thoroughbred horse.

Some of the finest touches of his humour are no doubt
much heightened by his perfect command of the genius
as well as the dialect of a peasantry, in whom a true
culture of mind and sometimes also of heart is found in
the closest possible contact with the humblest pursuits
and the quaintest enthusiasm for them.   But Scott, with
all his turn for irony—and Mr. Lockhart says that even on
his death-bed he used towards his children the same sort
of good-humoured irony to which he had always accustomed them in his life—certainly never gives us any
example of that highest irony which is found so frequently
in Shakespeare, which touches the paradoxes of the
spiritual life of the children of earth, and which reached
its highest point in Isaiah.   Now and then in his latest
diaries—the diaries written in his deep affliction—
he comes near the edge of it.   Once, for instance, he
says, " What a strange scene if the surge of conversation
could suddenly ebb like the tide, and show us the state of
people's real minds !

> ' No eyes the rocks discover
> Which lurk beneath the deep.'

Life could not be endured were it seen in reality."
But this is not irony, only the sort of meditation which,
in a mind inclined to thrust deep into the secrets of life's
paradoxes, is apt to lead to irony.   Scott, however, does
not thrust deep in this direction.   He met the cold steel
which inflicts the deepest interior wounds, like a soldier,
and never seems to have meditated on the higher paradoxes
of life till reason reeled.   The irony of Hamlet is far from
Scott.   His imagination was essentially one of distinct
embodiment.   He never even seemed so much as to con-
template that sundering of substance and form, that rending

away of outward garments, that unclothing of the soul, in order that it might be more effectually clothed upon, which is at the heart of anything that may be called spiritual irony. The constant abiding of his mind within the well-defined forms of some one or other of the conditions of outward life and manners, among the scores of different spheres of human habit, was, no doubt, one of the secrets of his genius; but it was also its greatest limitation.

## CHAPTER XI.

### MORALITY AND RELIGION.

THE very same causes which limited Scott's humour and irony to the commoner fields of experience, and prevented him from ever introducing into his stories characters of the highest type of moral thoughtfulness, gave to his own morality and religion, which were, I think, true to the core so far as they went, a shade of distinct conventionality. It is no doubt quite true, as he himself tells us, that he took more interest in his mercenaries and moss-troopers, outlaws, gipsies, and beggars, than he did in the fine ladies and gentlemen under a cloud whom he adopted as heroines and heroes. But that was the very sign of his conventionalism. Though he interested himself more in these irregular persons, he hardly ever ventured to paint their inner life so as to show how little there was to choose between the sins of those who are at war with society and the sins of those who bend to the yoke of society. He widened rather than narrowed the chasm between the outlaw and the respectable citizen, even while he did not disguise his own romantic interest in the former. He extenuated, no doubt, the sins of all brave and violent defiers of the law, as distinguished from the sins of crafty and cunning abusers of the law. But the leaning he had to the former was, as he was willing to

admit, what he regarded as a "naughty" leaning. He did
not attempt for a moment to balance accounts between
them and society. He paid his tribute as a matter of
course to the established morality, and only put in a word
or two by way of attempt to diminish the severity of the
sentence on the bold transgressor. And then, where what
is called the "law of honour" comes in to traverse the law
of religion, he had no scruple in setting aside the latter
in favour of the customs of gentlemen, without any
attempt to justify that course. Yet it is evident from
various passages in his writings that he held Christian
duty inconsistent with duelling, and that he held himself
a sincere Christian. In spite of this, when he was fifty-
six, and under no conceivable hurry or perturbation of
feeling, but only concerned to defend his own conduct
—which was indeed plainly right—as to a political dis-
closure which he had made in his life of Napoleon, he
asked his old friend William Clerk to be his second, if the
expected challenge from General Gourgaud should come,
and declared his firm intention of accepting it. On the
strength of official evidence he had exposed some conduct
of General Gourgaud's at St. Helena, which appeared to
be far from honourable, and he thought it his duty on
that account to submit to be shot at by General Gourgaud,
if General Gourgaud had wished it. In writing to William
Clerk to ask him to be his second, he says, "Like a
man who finds himself in a scrape, General Gourgaud may
wish to fight himself out of it, and if the quarrel should
be thrust on me, why, *I will not baulk him, Jackie.* He
shall not dishonour the country through my sides, I can
assure him." In other words, Scott acted just as he had
made Waverley and others of his heroes act, on a code of
honour which he knew to be false, and he must have felt

in this case to be something worse.  He thought himself
at that time under the most stringent obligations both to
his creditors and his children, to do all in his power to
redeem himself and his estate from debt.  Nay, more, he
held that his life was a trust from his Creator, which he
had no right to throw away merely because a man whom
he had not really injured, was indulging a strong wish to
injure him ; but he could so little brook the imputation of
physical cowardice, that he was moral coward enough to
resolve to meet General Gourgaud, if General Gourgaud
lusted after a shot at him.  Nor is there any trace preserved of so much as a moral scruple in his own mind on
the subject, and this though there are clear traces in his
other writings as to what he thought Christian morality
required.  But the Border chivalry was so strong in Scott
that, on subjects of this kind at least, his morality was
the conventional morality of a day rapidly passing
away.

He showed the same conventional feeling in his severity
towards one of his own brothers who had been guilty of
cowardice.  Daniel Scott was the black sheep of the
family.  He got into difficulties in business, formed a bad
connexion with an artful woman, and was sent to try his
fortunes in the West Indies.  There he was employed in
some service against a body of refractory negroes—we do
not know its exact nature—and apparently showed the
white feather.  Mr. Lockhart says that "he returned to
Scotland a dishonoured man; and though he found shelter
and compassion from his mother, his brother would never
see him again.  Nay, when, soon after, his health,
shattered by dissolute indulgence, . . . gave way altogether,
and he died, as yet a young man, the poet refused either
to attend his funeral or to wear mourning for him, like the

rest of his family." [1]   Indeed he always spoke of him as
his "relative," not as his brother.   Here again Scott's
severity was due to his brother's failure as a "man of
honour," i. e. in courage.   He was forbearing enough with
vices of a different kind ; made John Ballantyne's dissipa-
tion the object rather of his jokes than of his indignation;
and not only mourned for him, but really grieved for him
when he died.   It is only fair to say, however, that for
this conventional scorn of a weakness rather than a sin,
Scott sorrowed sincerely later in life, and that in sketching
the physical cowardice of Connochar in *The Fair Maid of
Perth*, he deliberately made an attempt to atone for this
hardness towards his brother by showing how frequently
the foundation of cowardice may be laid in perfectly
involuntary physical temperament, and pointing out with
what noble elements of disposition it may be combined.
But till reflection on many forms of human character had
enlarged Scott's charity, and perhaps also the range of his
speculative ethics, he remained a conventional moralist,
and one, moreover, the type of whose conventional code
was borrowed more from that of honour than from that of
religious principle.   There is one curious passage in his
diary, written very near the end of his life, in which
Scott even seems to declare that conventional standards of
conduct are better, or at least safer, than religious standards
of conduct.   He says in his diary for the 15th April,
1828,—"Dined with Sir Robert Inglis, and met Sir
Thomas Acland, my old and kind friend.   I was happy to
see him.   He may be considered now as the head of the
religious party in the House of Commons—a powerful
body which Wilberforce long commanded.   It is a difficult
situation, for the adaptation of religious motives to earthly

[1] Lockhart's *Life of Scott*, iii. 198-9.

policy is apt—among the infinite delusions of the human
heart—to be a snare." [1]    His letters to his eldest son,
the young cavalry officer, on his first start in life, are
much admired by Mr. Lockhart, but to me they read
a little hard, a little worldly, and extremely conventional.   Conventionality was certainly to his mind almost
a virtue.

Of enthusiasm in religion Scott always spoke very severely,
both in his novels and in his letters and private diary.
In writing to Lord Montague, he speaks of such enthusiasm
as was then prevalent at Oxford, and which makes, he says,
" religion a motive and a pretext for particular lines of
thinking in politics and in temporal affairs " [as if it could
help doing that!] as " teaching a new way of going to the
devil for God's sake," and this expressly, because when
the young are infected with it, it disunites families, and
sets " children in opposition to their parents." [2]   He gives
us, however, one reason for his dread of anything like enthusiasm, which is not conventional ;—that it interferes
with the submissive and tranquil mood which is the only
true religious mood.   Speaking in his diary of a weakness
and fluttering at the heart, from which he had suffered, he
says, " It is an awful sensation, and would have made an
enthusiast of me, had I indulged my imagination on religious subjects.   I have been always careful to place my
mind in the most tranquil posture which it can assume,
during my private exercises of devotion." [3]   And in this
avoidance of indulging the imagination on religious, or
even spiritual subjects, Scott goes far beyond Shakespeare.
I do not think there is a single study in all his romances

[1] Lockhart's *Life of Scott*, ix. 231.
[2] Ibid., vii. 255-6.          [3] Ibid., viii. 292.

of what may be fairly called a pre-eminently spiritual
character as such, though Jeanie Deans approaches nearest
to it.    The same may be said of Shakespeare.    But
Shakespeare, though he has never drawn a pre-eminently
spiritual character, often enough indulged his imagination
while meditating on spiritual themes.

## CHAPTER XII.

### DISTRACTIONS AND AMUSEMENTS AT ABBOTSFORD.

BETWEEN 1814 and the end of 1825, Scott's literary labour was interrupted only by one serious illness, and hardly interrupted by that,—by a few journeys,—one to Paris after the battle of Waterloo, and several to London, —and by the worry of a constant stream of intrusive visitors. Of his journeys he has left some records; but I cannot say that I think Scott would ever have reached, as a mere observer and recorder, at all the high point which he reached directly his imagination went to work to create a story. That imagination was, indeed, far less subservient to his mere perceptions than to his constructive powers. *Paul's Letters to his Kinsfolk*—the records of his Paris journey after Waterloo—for instance, are not at all above the mark of a good special correspondent. His imagination was less the imagination of insight, than the imagination of one whose mind was a great kaleidoscope of human life and fortunes. But far more interrupting than either illness or travel, was the lion-hunting of which Scott became the object, directly after the publication of the earlier novels. In great measure, no doubt, on account of the mystery as to his authorship, his fame became something oppressive. At one time as many as *sixteen* parties of visitors applied to see Abbotsford in a single day. Strangers,—especially the American travel-

lers of that day, who were much less reticent and more
irrepressible than the American travellers of this,—would
come to him without introductions, facetiously cry out
"Prodigious!" in imitation of Dominie Sampson, whatever they were shown, inquire whether the new house
was called Tullyveolan or Tillytudlem, cross-examine,
with open note-books, as to Scott's age, and the age of his
wife, and appear to be taken quite by surprise when they
were bowed out without being asked to dine.[1] In those
days of high postage Scott's bill for letters "seldom came
under 150l. a year," and "as to coach parcels, they were a
perfect ruination." On one occasion a mighty package
came by post from the United States, for which Scott had
to pay five pounds sterling. It contained a MS. play
called *The Cherokee Lovers*, by a young lady of New York,
who begged Scott to read and correct it, write a prologue
and epilogue, get it put on the stage at Drury Lane, and
negotiate with Constable or Murray for the copyright. In
about a fortnight another packet not less formidable
arrived, charged with a similar postage, which Scott, not
grown cautious through experience, recklessly opened; out
jumped a duplicate copy of *The Cherokee Lovers*, with a
second letter from the authoress, stating that as the weather had been stormy, and she feared that something
might have happened to her former MS., she had thought
it prudent to send him a duplicate.[2] Of course, when
fame reached such a point as this, it became both a worry
and a serious waste of money, and what was far more
valuable than money, of time, privacy, and tranquillity of
mind. And though no man ever bore such worries with
the equanimity of Scott, no man ever received less plea-

[1] Lockhart's *Life of Scott*, v. 387.
[2] Lockhart's *Life of Scott*, v. 382.

sure from the adulation of unknown and often vulgar and
ignorant admirers.  His real amusements were his trees
and his friends.  "Planting and pruning trees," he said,
" I could work at from morning to night.   There is a sort
of self-congratulation, a little tickling self-flattery, in the
idea that while you are pleasing and amusing yourself,
you are seriously contributing to the future welfare of
the country, and that your very acorn may send its future
ribs of oak to future victories like Trafalgar," [1]—for the
day of iron ships was not yet.   And again, at a later
stage of his planting :—" You can have no idea of the
exquisite delight of a planter,—he is like a painter laying
on his colours,—at every moment he sees his effects coming
out.   There is no art or occupation comparable to this ; it
is full of past, present, and future enjoyment.   I look
back to the time when there was not a tree here, only bare
heath ; I look round and see thousands of trees growing up,
all of which, I may say almost each of which, have received
my personal attention.   I remember, five years ago, looking forward with the most delighted expectation to this
very hour, and as each year has passed, the expectation
has gone on increasing.   I do the same now.   I anticipate
what this plantation and that one will presently be, if only
taken care of, and there is not a spot of which I do not
watch the progress.   Unlike building, or even painting, or
indeed any other kind of pursuit, this has no end, and
is never interrupted ; but goes on from day to day, and
from year to year, with a perpetually augmenting interest.
Farming I hate.   What have I to do with fattening
and killing beasts, or raising corn, only to cut it down,
and to wrangle with farmers about prices, and to be constantly at the mercy of the seasons ?   There can be no

[1]  Lockhart's *Life of Scott,* iii. 288.

such disappointments or annoyances in planting trees."[1]
Scott indeed regarded planting as a mode of so moulding
the form and colour of the outward world, that nature herself
became indebted to him for finer outlines, richer masses of
colour, and deeper shadows, as well as for more fertile and
sheltered soils.    And he was as skilful in producing the
last result, as he was in the artistic effects of his planting.    In the essay on the planting of waste lands, he
mentions a story,—drawn from his own experience,—of a
planter, who having scooped out the lowest part of his
land for enclosures, and " planted the wood round them in
masses enlarged or contracted as the natural lying of the
ground seemed to dictate," met, six years after these
changes, his former tenant on the ground, and said to him,
" I suppose, Mr. R——, you will say I have ruined your
farm by laying half of it into woodland?"  " I should have
expected it, sir," answered Mr. R——, " if you had told
me beforehand what you were going to do ; but I am now
of a very different opinion; and as I am looking for land
at present, if you are inclined to take for the remaining
sixty acres the same rent which I formerly gave for a hundred and twenty, I will give you an offer to that amount.
I consider the benefit of the enclosing, and the complete
shelter afforded to the fields, as an advantage which fairly
counterbalances the loss of one-half of the land."[2]

And Scott was not only thoughtful in his own
planting, but induced his neighbours to become so too.
So great was their regard for him, that many of them
planted their estates as much with reference to the effect
which their plantations would have on the view from
Abbotsford, as with reference to the effect they would

[1] Lockhart's *Life of Scott*, vii. 287-8.
[2] Scott's *Miscellaneous Prose Works*, xxi. 22-3.

have on the view from their own grounds.  Many was
the consultation which he and his neighbours, Scott of
Gala, for instance, and Mr. Henderson of Eildon Hall, had
together on the effect which would be produced on the
view from their respective houses, of the planting going on
upon the lands of each.  The reciprocity of feeling was
such that the various proprietors acted more like brothers
in this matter, than like the jealous and exclusive creatures
which landowners, as such, so often are.

Next to his interest in the management and growth
of his own little estate was Scott's interest in the management and growth of the Duke of Buccleuch's.  To the
Duke he looked up as the head of his clan, with something almost more than a feudal attachment, greatly
enhanced of course by the personal friendship which
he had formed for him in early life as the Earl of
Dalkeith.  This mixture of feudal and personal feeling
towards the Duke and Duchess of Buccleuch continued
during their lives.  Scott was away on a yachting tour
to the Shetlands and Orkneys in July and August, 1814,
and it was during this absence that the Duchess of
Buccleuch died.  Scott, who was in no anxiety about
her, employed himself in writing an amusing descriptive
epistle to the Duke in rough verse, chronicling his
voyage, and containing expressions of the profoundest
reverence for the goodness and charity of the Duchess,
a letter which did not reach its destination till after the
Duchess's death.  Scott himself heard of her death by
chance when they landed for a few hours on the coast of
Ireland; he was quite overpowered by the news, and went
to bed only to drop into short nightmare sleeps, and to
wake with the dim memory of some heavy weight at his
heart.  The Duke himself died five years later, leaving

a son only thirteen years of age (the present Duke), over whose interests, both as regarded his education and his estates, Scott watched as jealously as if they had been those of his own son.   Many were the anxious letters he wrote to Lord Montague as to his "young chief's" affairs, as he called them, and great his pride in watching the promise of his youth.   Nothing can be clearer than that to Scott the feudal principle was something far beyond a name ; that he had at least as much pride in his devotion to his chief, as he had in founding a house which he believed would increase the influence—both territorial and personal—of the clan of Scotts.   The unaffected reverence which he felt for the Duke, though mingled with warm personal affection, showed that Scott's feudal feeling had something real and substantial in it, which did not vanish even when it came into close contact with strong personal feelings.   This reverence is curiously marked in his letters.   He speaks of "the distinction of rank" being ignored by both sides, as of something quite exceptional, but it was never really ignored by him, for though he continued to write to the Duke as an intimate friend, it was with a mingling of awe, very different indeed from that which he ever adopted to Ellis or Erskine.   It is necessary to remember this, not only in estimating the strength of the feeling which made him so anxious to become himself the founder of a house within a house,— of a new branch of the clan of Scotts,—but in estimating the loyalty which Scott always displayed to one of the least respectable of English sovereigns, George IV.,—a matter of which I must now say a few words, not only because it led to Scott's receiving the baronetcy, but because it forms to my mind the most grotesque of all the threads in the lot of this strong and proud man.

## CHAPTER XIII.

### SCOTT AND GEORGE IV.

THE first relations of Scott with the Court were, oddly enough, formed with the Princess, not with the Prince of Wales.   In 1806 Scott dined with the Princess of Wales at Blackheath, and spoke of his invitation as a great honour. He wrote a tribute to her father, the Duke of Brunswick, in the introduction to one of the cantos of *Marmion*, and received from the Princess a silver vase in acknowledgment of this passage in the poem.   Scott's relations with the Prince Regent seem to have begun in an offer to Scott of the Laureateship in the summer of 1813, an offer which Scott would have found it very difficult to accept, so strongly did his pride revolt at the idea of having to commemorate in verse, as an official duty, all conspicuous incidents affecting the throne.   But he was at the time of the offer in the thick of his first difficulties on account of Messrs. John Ballantyne and Co., and it was only the Duke of Buccleuch's guarantee of 4000*l*.—a guarantee subsequently cancelled by Scott's paying the sum for which it was a security—that enabled him at this time to decline what, after Southey had accepted it, he compared in a letter to Southey to the herring for which the poor Scotch clergyman gave thanks in a grace wherein he described it as " even this, the very least of Providence's mercies."

In March, 1815, Scott being then in London, the Prince
Regent asked him to dinner, addressed him uniformly as
Walter, and struck up a friendship with him which seems
to have lasted their lives, and which certainly did much
more honour to George than to Sir Walter Scott. It is
impossible not to think rather better of George IV. for
thus valuing, and doing his best in every way to show his
value for, Scott. It is equally impossible not to think
rather worse of Scott for thus valuing, and in every way
doing his best to express his value for, this very worthless,
though by no means incapable king. The consequences
were soon seen in the indignation with which Scott began
to speak of the Princess of Wales's sins. In 1806, in the
squib he wrote on Lord Melville's acquittal, when im-
peached for corruption by the Liberal Government, he
had written thus of the Princess Caroline :—

> " Our King, too—our Princess,—I dare not say more, sir,—
>     May Providence watch them with mercy and might!
> While there's one Scottish hand that can wag a claymore, sir,
>     They shall ne'er want a friend to stand up for their right.
>             Be damn'd he that dare not—
>             For my part I'll spare not
>         To beauty afflicted a tribute to give ;
>             Fill it up steadily,
>             Drink it off readily,
>     Here's to the Princess, and long may she live."

But whoever " stood up " for the Princess's right, certainly
Scott did not do so after his intimacy with the Prince
Regent began. He mentioned her only with severity,
and in one letter at least, written to his brother, with
something much coarser than severity ;[1] but the king's
similar vices did not at all alienate him from what at

---

[1] Lockhart's *Life of Scott*, vi. 229-30.

least had all the appearance of a deep personal devotion to
his sovereign.   The first baronet whom George IV. made
on succeeding to the throne, after his long Regency, was
Scott, who not only accepted the honour gratefully, but
dwelt with extreme pride on the fact that it was offered to
him by the king himself, and was in no way due to the
prompting of any minister's advice.   He wrote to Joanna
Baillie on hearing of the Regent's intention—for the offer
was made by the Regent at the end of 1818, though it
was not actually conferred till after George's accession,
namely, on the 30th March, 1820,—"The Duke of
Buccleuch and Scott of Harden, who, as the heads of
my clan and the sources of my gentry, are good judges
of what I ought to do, have both given me their earnest
opinion to accept of an honour directly derived from the
source of honour, and neither begged nor bought, as is
the usual fashion.   Several of my ancestors bore the title
in the seventeenth century, and, were it of consequence,
I have no reason to be ashamed of the decent and respectable persons who connect me with that period when they
carried into the field, like Madoc,

> " The Crescent at whose gleam the Cambrian oft,
>   Cursing his perilous tenure, wound his horn,"

so that, as a gentleman, I may stand on as good a footing
as other new creations." [1]   Why the honour was any
greater for coming from such a king as George, than it
would have been if it had been suggested by Lord Sid-
mouth, or even Lord Liverpool,—or half as great as if
Mr. Canning had proposed it, it is not easy to conceive.
George was a fair judge of literary merit, but not one to

----

[1] Lockhart's *Life of Scott*, vi. 13, 14.

be compared for a moment with that great orator and wit;
and as to his being the fountain of honour, there was so
much dishonour of which the king was certainly the
fountain too, that I do not think it was very easy for two
fountains both springing from such a person to have flowed
quite unmingled.    George justly prided himself on Sir
Walter Scott's having been the first creation of his reign,
and I think the event showed that the poet was the fountain of much more honour for the king, than the king was
for the poet.

When George came to Edinburgh in 1822, it was Sir
Walter who acted virtually as the master of the ceremonies, and to whom it was chiefly due that the visit was
so successful.    It was then that George clad his substantial
person for the first time in the Highland costume—to wit,
in the Steuart Tartans—and was so much annoyed to find
himself outvied by a wealthy alderman, Sir William
Curtis, who had gone and done likewise, and, in his equally
grand Steuart Tartans, seemed a kind of parody of
the king.    The day on which the king arrived, Tuesday,
14th of August, 1822, was also the day on which Scott's
most intimate friend, William Erskine, then Lord Kinnedder, died.    Yet Scott went on board the royal yacht,
was most graciously received by George, had his health
drunk by the king in a bottle of Highland whiskey, and
with a proper show of devoted loyalty entreated to be
allowed to retain the glass out of which his Majesty had
just drunk his health.    The request was graciously acceded
to, but let it be pleaded on Scott's behalf, that on reaching
home and finding there his friend Crabbe the poet, he sat
down on the royal gift, and crushed it to atoms.    One
would hope that he was really thinking more even of
Crabbe, and much more of Erskine, than of the royal

favour for which he had appeared, and doubtless had
really believed himself, so grateful.  Sir Walter retained
his regard for the king, such as it was, to the last, and even
persuaded himself that George's death would be a great
political calamity for the nation.   And really I cannot help
thinking that Scott believed more in the king, than he did
in his friend George Canning.  Assuredly, greatly as he
admired Canning, he condemned him more and more as
Canning grew more liberal, and sometimes speaks of his
veerings in that direction with positive asperity.   George,
on the other hand, who believed more in number one than
in any other number, however large, became much more
conservative after he became Regent than he was before,
and as he grew more conservative Scott grew more conservative likewise, till he came to think this particular
king almost a pillar of the Constitution.   I suppose we
ought to explain this little bit of fetish-worship in Scott
much as we should the quaint practical adhesion to duelling
which he gave as an old man, who had had all his life
much more to do with the pen than the sword—that is, as
an evidence of the tendency of an improved type to recur
to that of the old wild stock on which it had been grafted.
But certainly no feudal devotion of his ancestors to their
chief was ever less justified by moral qualities than Scott's
loyal devotion to the fountain of honour as embodied in
"our fat friend."   The whole relation to George was a
grotesque thread in Scott's life ; and I cannot quite forgive
him for the utterly conventional severity with which he
threw over his first patron, the Queen, for sins which
were certainly not grosser, if they were not much less
gross, than those of his second patron, the husband who
had set her the example which she faithfully, though at a
distance, followed.

## CHAPTER XIV.

### SCOTT AS A POLITICIAN.

SCOTT usually professed great ignorance of politics, and did what he could to hold aloof from a world in which his feelings were very easily heated, while his knowledge was apt to be very imperfect.    But now and again, and notably towards the close of his life, he got himself mixed up in politics, and I need hardly say that it was always on the Tory, and generally on the red-hot Tory, side.    His first hasty intervention in politics was the song I have just referred to on Lord Melville's acquittal, during the short Whig administration of 1806.    In fact Scott's comparative abstinence from politics was due, I believe, chiefly to the fact that during almost the whole of his literary life, Tories and not Whigs were in power.    No sooner was any reform proposed, any abuse threatened, than Scott's eager Conservative spirit flashed up.    Proposals were made in 1806 for changes—and, as it was thought, reforms—in the Scotch Courts of Law, and Scott immediately saw something like national calamity in the prospect.    The mild proposals in question were discussed at a meeting of the Faculty of Advocates, when Scott made a speech longer than he had ever before delivered, and animated by a "flow and energy of eloquence" for which those who were accustomed to hear his debating speeches were quite unprepared.    He

walked home between two of the reformers, Mr. Jeffrey
and another, when his companions began to compliment
him on his eloquence, and to speak playfully of its
subject. But Scott was in no mood for playfulness.
" No, no," he exclaimed, " 'tis no laughing matter ; little
by little, whatever your wishes may be, you will destroy
and undermine, until nothing of what makes Scotland
Scotland shall remain !" "And so saying," adds Mr. Lockhart, " he turned round to conceal his agitation, but not
until Mr. Jeffrey saw tears gushing down his cheek,—resting his head, until he recovered himself, on the wall of the
Mound."[1] It was the same strong feeling for old Scotch
institutions which broke out so quaintly in the midst of his
own worst troubles in 1826, on behalf of the Scotch bank-
ing-system, when he so eloquently defended, in the letters
of *Malachi Malagrowther*, what would now be called
Home-Rule for Scotland, and indeed really defeated the
attempt of his friends the Tories, who were the innovators
this time, to encroach on those sacred institutions—the
Scotch one-pound note, and the private-note circulation of
the Scotch banks. But when I speak of Scott as a Home-
Ruler, I should add that had not Scotland been for generations governed to a great extent, and, as he thought
successfully, by Home-Rule, he was far too good a Conservative to have apologized for it at all. The basis of his
Conservatism was always the danger of undermining a
system which had answered so well. In the concluding
passages of the letters to which I have just referred, he
contrasts " Theory, a scroll in her hand, full of deep and
mysterious combinations of figures, the least failure in
any one of which may alter the result entirely," with

---

[1] Lockhart's *Life of Scott*, ii. 328.

"a practical system successful for upwards of a century."
His vehement and unquailing opposition to Reform in
almost the very last year of his life, when he had already
suffered more than one stroke of paralysis, was grounded
on precisely the same argument. At Jedburgh, on the
21st March, 1831, he appeared in the midst of an angry
population (who hooted and jeered at him till he turned
round fiercely upon them with the defiance, "I regard your
gabble no more than the geese on the green," to urge the
very same protest. "We in this district," he said, "are
proud, and with reason, that the first chain-bridge was the
work of a Scotchman. It still hangs where he erected
it a pretty long time ago. The French heard of our
invention, and determined to introduce it, but with
great improvements and embellishments. A friend of
my own saw the thing tried. It was on the Seine at
Marly. The French chain-bridge looked lighter and
airier than the prototype. Every Englishman present
was disposed to confess that we had been beaten at our
own trade. But by-and-by the gates were opened, and
the multitude were to pass over. It began to swing
rather formidably beneath the pressure of the good company ; and by the time the architect, who led the procession in great pomp and glory, reached the middle, the
whole gave way, and he—worthy, patriotic artist—was
the first that got a ducking. They had forgot the middle
bolt,—or rather this ingenious person had conceived that
to be a clumsy-looking feature, which might safely be
dispensed with, while he put some invisible gimcrack of
his own to supply its place." [1] It is strange that Sir
Walter did not see that this kind of criticism, so far as it

---

[1] Lockhart's *Life of Scott*, x. 47.

applied at all to such an experiment as the Reform Bill,
was even more in point as a rebuke to the rashness of the
Scotch reformer who hung the first successful chain-bridge,
than to the rashness of the French reformer of reform who
devised an unsuccessful variation on it.   The audacity of
the first experiment was much the greater, though the com-
petence of the person who made it was the greater also.
And as a matter of fact, the political structure against the
supposed insecurity of which Sir Walter was protesting,
with all the courage of that dauntless though dying nature,
was made by one who understood his work at least as well
as the Scotch architect.   The tramp of the many multi-
tudes who have passed over it has never yet made it to
" swing dangerously," and Lord Russell in the fulness of
his age was but yesterday rejoicing in what he had achieved,
and even in what those have achieved who have altered
his work in the same spirit in which he designed it.

But though Sir Walter persuaded himself that his
Conservatism was all founded in legitimate distrust of
reckless change, there is evidence, I think, that at times
at least it was due to elements less noble.   The least
creditable incident in the story of his political life—which
Mr. Lockhart, with his usual candour, did not conceal—
was the bitterness with which he resented a most natural
and reasonable Parliamentary opposition to an appointment which he had secured for his favourite brother, Tom.
In 1810 Scott appointed his brother Tom, who had failed
as a Writer to the Signet, to a place vacant under himself
as Clerk of Session.   He had not given him the best place
vacant, because he thought it his duty to appoint an
official who had grown grey in the service, but he gave
Tom Scott this man's place, which was worth about 250*l.*
a year.   In the meantime Tom Scott's affairs did not

render it convenient for him to be come-at-able, and he
absented himself, while they were being settled, in the
Isle of Man.   Further, the Commission on the Scotch
system of judicature almost immediately reported that his
office was one of supererogation, and ought to be abolished ;
but, to soften the blow, they proposed to allow him a
pension of 130*l.* per annum.   This proposal was discussed with some natural jealousy in the House of Lords.
Lord Lauderdale thought that when Tom Scott was
appointed, it must have been pretty evident that the
Commission would propose to abolish his office, and that
the appointment therefore should not have been made.
" Mr. Thomas Scott," he said, " would have 130*l.* for life
as an indemnity for an office the duties of which he never
had performed, while those clerks who had laboured for
twenty years had no adequate remuneration."   Lord Holland supported this very reasonable and moderate view of
the case ; but of course the Ministry carried their way,
and Tom Scott got his unearned pension.   Nevertheless,
Scott was furious with Lord Holland.   Writing soon after
to the happy recipient of this little pension, he says,
" Lord Holland has been in Edinburgh, and we met acci-
dentally at a public party.   He made up to me, but I
remembered his part in your affair, and *cut* him with as
little remorse as an old pen."   Mr. Lockhart says, on
Lord Jeffrey's authority, that the scene was a very painful
one.   Lord Jeffrey himself declared that it was the only
rudeness of which he ever saw Scott guilty in the course
of a life-long familiarity.   And it is pleasant to know that
he renewed his cordiality with Lord Holland in later years,
though there is no evidence that he ever admitted that he
had been in the wrong.   But the incident shows how
very doubtful Sir Walter ought to have felt as to the purity

of his Conservatism. It is quite certain that the proposal to abolish Tom Scott's office without compensation was not a reckless experiment of a fundamental kind. It was a mere attempt at diminishing the heavy burdens laid on the people for the advantage of a small portion of the middle class, and yet Scott resented it with as much display of selfish passion—considering his genuine nobility of breeding—as that with which the rude working men of Jedburgh afterwards resented his gallant protest against the Reform Bill, and, later again, saluted the dauntless old man with the dastardly cry of " Burk Sir Walter ! " Judged truly, I think Sir Walter's conduct in cutting Lord Holland " with as little remorse as an old pen," for simply doing his duty in the House of Lords, was quite as ignoble in him as the bullying and insolence of the democratic party in 1831, when the dying lion made his last dash at what he regarded as the foes of the Constitution. Doubtless he held that the mob, or, as we more decorously say, the residuum, were in some sense the enemies of true freedom. " I cannot read in history," he writes once to Mr. Laidlaw, " of any free State which has been brought to slavery till the rascal and uninstructed populace had had their short hour of anarchical government, which naturally leads to the stern repose of military despotism." But he does not seem ever to have perceived that educated men identify themselves with " the rascal and uninstructed populace," whenever they indulge on behalf of the selfish interests of their own class, passions such as he had indulged in fighting for his brother's pension. It is not the want of instruction, it is the rascaldom, i. e. the violent *esprit de corps* of a selfish class, which " naturally leads " to violent remedies. Such rascaldom exists in all classes, and not

least in the class of the cultivated and refined. Generous
and magnanimous as Scott was, he was evidently by no
means free from the germs of it.

One more illustration of Scott's political Conservatism,
and I may leave his political life, which was not indeed his
strong side, though, as with all sides of Scott's nature, it
had an energy and spirit all his own. On the subject of
Catholic Emancipation he took a peculiar view. As he
justly said, he hated bigotry, and would have left the
Catholics quite alone, but for the great claims of their
creed to interfere with political life. And even so, when
the penal laws were once abolished, he would have
abolished also the representative disabilities, as quite
useless, as well as very irritating when the iron system of
effective repression had ceased. But he disapproved of the
abolition of the political parts of the penal laws. He
thought they would have stamped out Roman Catholicism ;
and whether that were just or unjust, he thought it would
have been a great national service. " As for Catholic
Emancipation," he wrote to Southey in 1807, " I am not,
God knows, a bigot in religious matters, nor a friend to
persecution ; but if a particular set of religionists are *ipso
facto* connected with foreign politics, and placed under
the spiritual direction of a class of priests, whose unrivalled
dexterity and activity are increased by the rules which
detach them from the rest of the world—I humbly think
that we may be excused from entrusting to them those
places in the State where the influence of such a clergy,
who act under the direction of a passive tool of our worst
foe, is likely to be attended with the most fatal consequences. If a gentleman chooses to walk about with a
couple of pounds of gunpowder in his pocket, if I give
him the shelter of my roof, I may at least be permitted

L

to exclude him from the seat next to the fire." [1]   And in
relation to the year 1825, when Scott visited Ireland, Mr.
Lockhart writes, "He on all occasions expressed manfully
his belief that the best thing for Ireland would have been
never to relax the strictly *political* enactments of the penal
laws, however harsh these might appear.  Had they been
kept in vigour for another half-century, it was his conviction that Popery would have been all but extinguished in
Ireland.  But he thought that after admitting Romanists
to the elective franchise, it was a vain notion that they
could be permanently or advantageously deterred from
using that franchise in favour of those of their own per-
suasion."

In his diary in 1829 he puts the same view still more
strongly :—"I cannot get myself to feel at all anxious
about the Catholic question.  I cannot see the use of
fighting about the platter, when you have let them snatch
the meat off it.  I hold Popery to be such a mean and
degrading superstition, that I am not sure I could have
found myself liberal enough for voting the repeal of the
penal laws as they existed before 1780.  They must and
would, in course of time, have smothered Popery ; and I
confess that I should have seen the old lady of Babylon's
mouth stopped with pleasure.  But now that you have
taken the plaster off her mouth, and given her free respi-
ration, I cannot see the sense of keeping up the irritation
about the claim to sit in Parliament.  Unopposed, the
Catholic superstition may sink into dust, with all its
absurd ritual and solemnities.  Still it is an awful risk.
The world is in fact as silly as ever, and a good compe-
tence of nonsense will always find believers." [2]   That is

[1] Lockhart's *Life of Scott*, iii. 34.
[2] Ibid., ix. 305.

the view of a strorg and rather unscrupulous politician
—a moss-trooper in politics —which Scott certainly
was.   He was thinking evidently very little of justice,
almost entirely of the most effective means of keeping
the Kingdom, the Kingdom which he loved.   Had he
understood—what none of the politicians of that day
understood—the strength of the Church of Rome as the
only consistent exponent of the principle of Authority
in religion, I believe his opposition to Catholic emancipation would have been as bitter as his opposition
to Parliamentary reform.   But he took for granted that
while only "silly" persons believed in Rome, and only
"infidels" rejected an authoritative creed altogether, it
was quite easy by the exercise of common sense, to find
the true compromise between reason and religious humility.
Had Scott lived through the religious controversies of our
own days, it seems not unlikely that with his vivid imagination, his warm Conservatism, and his rather inadequate
critical powers, he might himself have become a Roman
Catholic.

## CHAPTER XV.

### SCOTT IN ADVERSITY.

WITH the year 1825 came a financial crisis, and Constable began to tremble for his solvency. From the date of his baronetcy Sir Walter had launched out into a considerable increase of expenditure. He got plans on a rather large scale in 1821 for the increase of Abbotsford, which were all carried out. To meet his expenses in this and other ways he received Constable's bills for "four unnamed works of fiction," of which he had not written a line, but which came to exist in time, and were called *Peveril of the Peak, Quentin Durward, St. Ronan's Well,* and *Redgauntlet.* Again, in the very year before the crash, 1825, he married his eldest son, the heir to the title, to a young lady who was herself an heiress, Miss Jobson of Lochore, when Abbotsford and its estates were settled, with the reserve of 10,000*l.*, which Sir Walter took power to charge on the property for purposes of business. Immediately afterwards he purchased a captaincy in the King's Hussars for his son, which cost him 3500*l.* Nor were the obligations he incurred on his own account, or that of his family, the only ones by which he was burdened. He was always incurring expenses, often heavy expenses, for other people. Thus, when Mr. Terry, the actor, became joint lessee and manager of the Adelphi

Theatre, London, Scott became his surety for 1250*l.*, while
James Ballantyne became his surety for 500*l.* more, and
both these sums had to be paid by Sir Walter after
Terry's failure in 1828.    Such obligations as these, however, would have been nothing when compared with Sir
Walter's means, had all his bills on Constable been duly
honoured, and had not the printing firm of Ballantyne
and Co. been so deeply involved with Constable's house
that it necessarily became insolvent when he stopped.
Taken altogether, I believe that Sir Walter earned during
his own lifetime at least 140,000*l.* by his literary work
alone, probably more; while even on his land and building
combined he did not apparently spend more than half
that sum.    Then he had a certain income, about 1000*l.* a
year, from his own and Lady Scott's private property, as
well as 1300*l.* a year as Clerk of Session, and 300*l.* more
as Sheriff of Selkirk.    Thus even his loss of the price
of several novels by Constable's failure would not
seriously have compromised Scott's position, but for his
share in the printing-house which fell with Constable,
and the obligations of which amounted to 117,000*l.*

  As Scott had always forestalled his income,—spending the purchase-money of his poems and novels before
they were written,—such a failure as this, at the age
of fifty-five, when all the freshness of his youth was
gone out of him, when he saw his son's prospects blighted
as well as his own, and knew perfectly that James
Ballantyne, unassisted by him, could never hope to pay
any fraction of the debt worth mentioning, would have
been paralysing, had he not been a man of iron nerve,
and of a pride and courage hardly ever equalled.    Domestic calamity, too, was not far off.    For two years he had
been watching the failure of his wife's health with in-

creasing anxiety, and as calamities seldom come single, her illness took a most serious form at the very time when the blow fell, and she died within four months of the failure. Nay, Scott was himself unwell at the critical moment, and was taking sedatives which discomposed his brain. Twelve days before the final failure,—which was announced to him on the 17th January, 1826,—he enters in his diary, " Much alarmed. I had walked till twelve with Skene and Russell, and then sat down to my work. To my horror and surprise I could neither write nor spell, but put down one word for another, and wrote nonsense. I was much overpowered at the same time and could not conceive the reason. I fell asleep, however, in my chair, and slept for two hours. On my waking my head was clearer, and I began to recollect that last night I had taken the anodyne left for the purpose by Clarkson, and being disturbed in the course of the night, I had not slept it off." In fact the hyoscyamus had, combined with his anxieties, given him a slight attack of what is now called *aphasia*, that brain disease the most striking symptom of which is that one word is mis-taken for another. And this was Scott's preparation for his failure, and the bold resolve which followed it, to work for his creditors as he had worked for himself, and to pay off, if possible, the whole 117,000*l.* by his own literary exertions.

There is nothing in its way in the whole of English biography more impressive than the stoical extracts from Scott's diary which note the descent of this blow. Here is the anticipation of the previous day : " Edinburgh, January 16th.—Came through cold roads to as cold news. Hurst and Robinson have suffered a bill to come back upon Constable, which, I suppose, infers the ruin of both houses.

We shall soon see.  Dined with the Skenes."  And here
is the record itself: "January 17th.—James Ballantyne
this morning, good honest fellow, with a visage as black
as the crook.  He hopes no salvation ; has, indeed, taken
measures to stop.  It is hard, after having fought such a
battle.  I have apologized for not attending the Royal
Society Club, who have a *gaudeamus* on this day, and
seemed to count much on my being the præses.  My old
acquaintance Miss Elizabeth Clerk, sister of Willie, died
suddenly.  I cannot choose but wish it had been Sir
W. S., and yet the feeling is unmanly.  I have Anne,
my wife, and Charles to look after.  I felt rather sneaking as I came home from the Parliament-house—felt as if
I were liable *monstrari digito* in no very pleasant way.
But this must be borne *cum cæteris ;* and, thank God,
however uncomfortable, I do not feel despondent."[1]  On
the following day, the 18th January, the day after the
blow, he records a bad night, a wish that the next two
days were over, but that "the worst *is* over," and on
the same day he set about making notes for the *magnum
opus*, as he called it—the complete edition of all the
novels, with a new introduction and notes.  On the 19th
January, two days after the failure, he calmly resumed the
composition of *Woodstock*—the novel on which he was
then engaged—and completed, he says, "about twenty
printed pages of it;" to which he adds that he had "a
painful scene after dinner and another after supper,
endeavouring to convince these poor creatures " [his wife
and daughter] "that they must not look for miracles, but
consider the misfortune as certain, and only to be lessened
by patience and labour."  On the 21st January, after a

Lockhart's *Life of Scott*, viii. 197.

number of business details, he quotes from Job, "Naked
we entered the world and naked we leave it; blessed be
the name of the Lord." On the 22nd he says, "I feel
neither dishonoured nor broken down by the bad, now
truly bad, news I have received. I have walked my last
in the domains I have planted—sat the last time in the
halls I have built. But death would have taken them
from me, if misfortune had spared them. My poor people
whom I loved so well! There is just another die to turn
up against me in this run of ill-luck, i. e. if I should break
my magic wand in the fall from this elephant, and lose
my popularity with my fortune. Then *Woodstock* and
*Boney*" [his life of Napoleon] "may both go to the
paper-maker, and I may take to smoking cigars and
drinking grog, or turn devotee and intoxicate the brain
another way."[1] He adds that when he sets to work
doggedly, he is exactly the same man he ever was, "neither
low-spirited nor *distrait*," nay, that adversity is to him
"a tonic and bracer."

The heaviest blow was, I think, the blow to his pride.
Very early he begins to note painfully the different way in
which different friends greet him, to remark that some
smile as if to say, "think nothing about it, my lad, it is
quite out of our thoughts;" that others adopt an affected
gravity, "such as one sees and despises at a funeral," and
the best-bred "just shook hands and went on." He writes
to Mr. Morritt with a proud indifference, clearly to some
extent simulated :—"My womenkind will be the greater
sufferers, yet even they look cheerily forward; and, for
myself, the blowing off of my hat on a stormy day has
given me more uneasiness."[2] To Lady Davy he writes

---

[1] Lockhart's *Life of Scott*, viii. 203-4.
[2] Ibid., viii. 235.

truly enough :—"I beg my humblest compliments to Sir
Humphrey, and tell him, Ill Luck, that direful chemist,
never put into his crucible a more indissoluble piece of
stuff than your affectionate cousin and sincere well-
wisher, Walter Scott." [1]   When his *Letters of Malachi
Malagrowther* came out he writes:—"I am glad of this
bruilzie, as far as I am concerned; people will not dare
talk of me as an object of pity—no more ' poor-manning.'
Who asks how many punds Scots the old champion had
in his pocket when

> ' He set a bugle to his mouth,
>    And blew so loud and shrill,
>  The trees in greenwood shook thereat,
>    Sae loud rang every hill.'

This sounds conceited enough, yet is not far from truth." [2]
His dread of pity is just the same when his wife dies :—
" Will it be better," he writes, "when left to my own
feelings, I see the whole world pipe and dance around
me ?  I think it will.  Their sympathy intrudes on my
present affliction."   Again, on returning for the first time
from Edinburgh to Abbotsford after Lady Scott's funeral:—
" I again took possession of the family bedroom and my
widowed couch.  This was a sore trial, but it was necessary not to blink such a resolution.  Indeed I do not like
to have it thought that there is any way in which I can
be beaten."    And again:—" I have a secret pride—I
fancy it will be so most truly termed—which impels me to
mix with my distresses strange snatches of mirth, ' which
have no mirth in them.' " [3]

[1] Lockhart's *Life of Scott*, viii. 238.
[2] viii. 277.                    [3] viii., 347, 371, 381.

But though pride was part of Scott's strength, pride
alone never enabled any man to struggle so vigorously and
so unremittingly as he did to meet the obligations he had
incurred.   When he was in Ireland in the previous year,
a poor woman who had offered to sell him gooseberries,
but whose offer had not been accepted, remarked, on
seeing his daughter give some pence to a beggar, that they
might as well give her an alms too, as she was "an old
struggler."  Sir Walter was struck with the expression,
and said that it deserved to become classical, as a name
for those who take arms against a sea of troubles, instead of yielding to the waves.  It was certainly a name
the full meaning of which he himself deserved.   His
house in Edinburgh was sold, and he had to go into
a certain Mrs. Brown's lodgings, when he was discharging his duties as Clerk of Session.  His wife was
dead.   His estate was conveyed to trustees for the benefit
of his creditors till such time as he should pay off
Ballantyne and Co's. debt, which of course in his lifetime
he never did.   Yet between January, 1826, and January,
1828, he earned for his creditors very nearly 40,000*l.*
*Woodstock* sold for 8228*l.*, "a matchless sale," as Sir
Walter remarked, "for less than three months' work."
The first two editions of *The Life of Napoleon Bona-
parte*, on which Mr. Lockhart says that Scott had spent
the unremitting labour of about two years—labour involving a far greater strain on eyes and brain than his
imaginative work ever caused him—sold for 18,000*l.*
Had Sir Walter's health lasted, he would have redeemed
his obligations on behalf of Ballantyne and Co. within
eight or nine years at most from the time of his failure.
But what is more remarkable still, is that after his health
failed he struggled on with little more than half a brain,

but a whole will, to work while it was yet day, though the evening was dropping fast. *Count Robert of Paris* and *Castle Dangerous* were really the compositions of a paralytic patient.

It was in September, 1830, that the first of these tales was begun. As early as the 15th February of that year he had had his first true paralytic seizure. He had been discharging his duties as clerk of session as usual, and received in the afternoon a visit from a lady friend of his, Miss Young, who was submitting to him some manuscript memoirs of her father, when the stroke came. It was but slight. He struggled against it with his usual iron power of will, and actually managed to stagger out of the room where the lady was sitting with him, into the drawing-room where his daughter was, but there he fell his full length on the floor. He was cupped, and fully recovered his speech during the course of the day, but Mr. Lockhart thinks that never, after this attack, did his style recover its full lucidity and terseness. A cloudiness in words and a cloudiness of arrangement began to be visible. In the course of the year he retired from his duties of clerk of session, and his publishers hoped that, by engaging him on the new and complete edition of his works, they might detach him from the attempt at imaginative creation for which he was now so much less fit. But Sir Walter's will survived his judgment. When, in the previous year, Ballantyne had been disabled from attending to business by his wife's illness (which ended in her death), Scott had written in his diary, " It is his (Ballantyne's) nature to indulge apprehensions of the worst which incapacitate him for labour. I cannot help regarding this amiable weakness of the mind with something too nearly allied to contempt," and assuredly he

was guilty of no such weakness himself. Not only did
he row much harder against the stream of fortune than he
had ever rowed with it, but, what required still more
resolution, he fought on against the growing conviction
that his imagination would not kindle, as it used to do,
to its old heat.

When he dictated to Laidlaw,—for at this time he could
hardly write himself for rheumatism in the hand,—he
would frequently pause and look round him, like a man
" mocked with shadows." Then he bestirred himself with
a great effort, rallied his force, and the style again flowed
clear and bright, but not for long. The clouds would
gather again, and the mental blank recur. This soon
became visible to his publishers, who wrote discouragingly
of the new novel—to Scott's own great distress and irritation. The oddest feature in the matter was that his
letters to them were full of the old terseness, and force,
and caustic turns. On business he was as clear and keen
as in his best days. It was only at his highest task, the
task of creative work, that his cunning began to fail him.
Here, for instance, are a few sentences written to Cadell,
his publisher, touching this very point—the discouragement which James Ballantyne had been pouring on the
new novel. Ballantyne, he says, finds fault with the
subject, when what he really should have found fault with
was the failing power of the author :—" James is, with
many other kindly critics, perhaps in the predicament of
an honest drunkard, when crop-sick the next morning,
who does not ascribe the malady to the wine he has
drunk, but to having tasted some particular dish at dinner
which disagreed with his stomach. . . . . I have lost, it
is plain, the power of interesting the country, and ought,
in justice to all parties, to retire while I have some credit.

But this is an important step, and I will not be obstinate
about it if it be necessary. . . . . Frankly, I cannot think
of flinging aside the half-finished volume, as if it were a
corked bottle of wine. . . . . I may, perhaps, take a trip
to the Continent for a year or two, if I find Othello's
occupation gone, or rather Othello's *reputation*."[1]  And
again, in a very able letter written on the 12th of December, 1830, to Cadell, he takes a view of the situation
with as much calmness and imperturbability as if he were
an outside spectator.  "There were many circumstances in
the matter which you and J. B. (James Ballantyne) could
not be aware of, and which, if you were aware of, might
have influenced your judgment, which had, and yet have,
a most powerful effect upon mine.  The deaths of both
my father and mother have been preceded by a paralytic
shock.  My father survived it for nearly two years—a
melancholy respite, and not to be desired.  I was
alarmed with Miss Young's morning visit, when, as you
know, I lost my speech.  The medical people said it
was from the stomach, which might be, but while
there is a doubt upon a point so alarming, you will not
wonder that the subject, or to use Hare's *lingo*, the *shot*,
should be a little anxious."  He relates how he had
followed all the strict medical *régime* prescribed to him
with scrupulous regularity, and then begun his work
again with as much attention as he could.  "And having
taken pains with my story, I find it is not relished,
nor indeed tolerated, by those who have no interest in
condemning it, but a strong interest in putting even a
face " (? force) " upon their consciences.  Was not this,
in the circumstances, a damper to an invalid already

<hr>

[1]  Lockhart's *Life of Scott*, x. 11, 12.

afraid that the sharp edge might be taken off his intellect, though he was not himself sensible of that ?" In
fact, no more masterly discussion of the question whether
his mind were failing or not, and what he ought to do in
the interval of doubt, can be conceived, than these letters
give us.  At this time the debt of Ballantyne and Co. had
been reduced by repeated dividends—all the fruits of
Scott's literary work—more than one half.  On the 17th
of December, 1830, the liabilities stood at 54,000l.,
having been reduced 63,000l. within five years.  And Sir
Walter, encouraged by this great result of his labour,
resumed the suspended novel.

But with the beginning of 1831 came new alarms.  On
January 5th Sir Walter enters in his diary,—" Very
indifferent, with more awkward feelings than I can well
bear up against.  My voice sunk and my head strangely
confused."  Still he struggled on.  On the 31st January
he went alone to Edinburgh to sign his will, and stayed
at his bookseller's (Cadell's) house in Athol Crescent.
A great snow-storm set in which kept him in Edinburgh and in Mr. Cadell's house till the 9th February.
One day while the snow was still falling heavily, Ballantyne reminded him that a motto was wanting for
one of the chapters of *Count Robert of Paris*.  He
went to the window, looked out for a moment, and then
wrote,—

> " The storm increases ; 'tis no sunny shower,
>   Foster'd in the moist breast of March or April,
>   Or such as parchèd summer cools his lips with.
>   Heaven's windows are flung wide ; the inmost deeps
>   Call, in hoarse greeting, one upon another ;
>   On comes the flood, in all its foaming horrors,
>   And where's the dike shall stop it ?
>                             *The Deluge : a Poem.*"

Clearly this failing imagination of Sir Walter's was still
a great deal more vivid than that of most men, with
brains as sound as it ever pleased Providence to make
them. But his troubles were not yet even numbered.
The "storm increased," and it was, as he said, "no sunny
shower." His lame leg became so painful that he had to
get a mechanical apparatus to relieve him of some of the
burden of supporting it. Then, on the 21st March, he
was hissed at Jedburgh, as I have before said, for his
vehement opposition to Reform. In April he had another
stroke of paralysis which he now himself recognized as
one. Still he struggled on at his novel. Under the date
of May 6, 7, 8, he makes this entry in his diary :—"Here
is a precious job. I have a formal remonstrance from those
critical people, Ballantyne and Cadell, against the last
volume of *Count Robert*, which is within a sheet of being
finished. I suspect their opinion will be found to coincide
with that of the public ; at least it is not very different
from my own. The blow is a stunning one, I suppose,
for I scarcely feel it. It is singular, but it comes with
as little surprise as if I had a remedy ready ; yet God
knows I am at sea in the dark, and the vessel leaky, I
think, into the bargain. I cannot conceive that I have
tied a knot with my tongue which my teeth cannot untie.
We shall see. I have suffered terribly, that is the truth,
rather in body than mind, and I often wish I could lie
down and sleep without waking. But I will fight it out
if I can."[1] The medical men with one accord tried to
make him give up his novel-writing. But he smiled and
put them by. He took up *Count Robert of Paris* again,
and tried to recast it. On the 18th May he insisted on

---

[1] Lockhart's *Life of Scott*, x. 65-6.

attending the election for Roxburghshire, to be held at
Jedburgh, and in spite of the unmannerly reception he
had met with in March, no dissuasion would keep him at
home.   He was saluted in the town with groans and
blasphemies, and Sir Walter had to escape from Jedburgh
by a back way to avoid personal violence.   The cries
of "Burk Sir Walter," with which he was saluted on this
occasion, haunted him throughout his illness and on his
dying bed.   At the Selkirk election it was Sir Walter's
duty as Sheriff to preside, and his family therefore made
no attempt to dissuade him from his attendance.   There
he was so well known and loved, that in spite of his Tory
views, he was not insulted, and the only man who made
any attempt to hustle the Tory electors, was seized by Sir
Walter with his own hand, as he got out of his carriage,
and committed to prison without resistance till the election
day was over.

A seton which had been ordered for his head, gave him
some relief, and of course the first result was that he
turned immediately to his novel-writing again, and began
*Castle Dangerous* in July, 1831,—the last July but one
which he was to see at all.   He even made a little
journey in company with Mr. Lockhart, in order to see
the scene of the story he wished to tell, and on his return
set to work with all his old vigour to finish his tale,
and put the concluding touches to *Count Robert of Paris*.
But his temper was no longer what it had been.   He
quarrelled with Ballantyne, partly for his depreciatory
criticism of *Count Robert of Paris*, partly for his growing
tendency to a mystic and strait-laced sort of dissent and
his increasing Liberalism.   Even Mr. Laidlaw and Scott's
children had much to bear.   But he struggled on even to
the end, and did not consent to try the experiment of a

voyage and visit to Italy till his immediate work was done.
Well might Lord Chief Baron Shepherd apply to Scott
Cicero's description of some contemporary of his own, who
"had borne adversity wisely, who had not been broken by
fortune, and who, amidst the buffets of fate, had main-
tained his dignity." There was in Sir Walter, I think,
at least as much of the Stoic as the Christian. But
Stoic or Christian, he was a hero of the old, indomitable
type. Even the last fragments of his imaginative power
were all turned to account by that unconquerable will,
amidst the discouragement of friends, and the still more
disheartening doubts of his own mind. Like the head-
land stemming a rough sea, he was gradually worn away,
but never crushed.

## CHAPTER XVI.

THE LAST YEAR.

IN the month of September, 1831, the disease of the
brain which had long been in existence must have made
a considerable step in advance.  For the first time the
illusion seemed to possess Sir Walter that he had paid
off all the debt for which he was liable, and that he was
once more free to give as his generosity prompted.  Scott
sent Mr. Lockhart 50*l.* to save his grandchildren some
slight inconvenience, and told another of his corre-
spondents that he had "put his decayed fortune into as
good a condition as he could desire."  It was well, therefore, that he had at last consented to try the effect of
travel on his health,—not that he could hope to arrest
by it such a disease as his, but that it diverted him from
the most painful of all efforts, that of trying anew the
spell which had at last failed him, and perceiving in the
disappointed eyes of his old admirers that the magic of
his imagination was a thing of the past.  The last day
of real enjoyment at Abbotsford—for when Sir Walter
returned to it to die, it was but to catch once more the
outlines of its walls, the rustle of its woods, and the
gleam of its waters, through senses already darkened to
all less familiar and less fascinating visions—was the
22nd September, 1831.  On the 21st, Wordsworth had

XVI.] THE LAST YEAR. 163

come to bid his old friend adieu, and on the 22nd—the last
day at home—they spent the morning together in a visit
to Newark. It was a day to deepen alike in Scott and
in Wordsworth whatever of sympathy either of them had
with the very different genius of the other, and that it
had this result in Wordsworth's case, we know from the
very beautiful poem,—" Yarrow Revisited,"—and the son-
net which the occasion also produced. And even Scott,
who was so little of a Wordsworthian, who enjoyed
Johnson's stately but formal verse, and Crabbe's vivid
Dutch painting, more than he enjoyed the poetry of the
transcendental school, must have recurred that day with
more than usual emotion to his favourite Wordsworthian
poem. Soon after his wife's death, he had remarked in
his diary how finely " the effect of grief upon persons who
like myself are highly susceptible of humour " had been
" touched by Wordsworth in the character of the merry
village teacher, Matthew, whom Jeffrey profanely calls
a half-crazy, sentimental person." [1] And long before this
time, during the brightest period of his life, Scott had
made the old Antiquary of his novel quote the same
poem of Wordsworth's, in a passage where the period of
life at which he had now arrived is anticipated with
singular pathos and force. " It is at such moments as
these," says Mr. Oldbuck, " that we feel the changes of
time. The same objects are before us—those inanimate
things which we have gazed on in wayward infancy and
impetuous youth, in anxious and scheming manhood—they
are permanent and the same; but when we look upon
them in cold, unfeeling old age, can we, changed in our
temper, our pursuits, our feelings,—changed in our form,
our limbs, and our strength,—can we be ourselves called the

---

[1] Lockhart's *Life of Scott*, ix. 63.

M 2

same ? or do we not rather look back with a sort of wonder
upon our former selves as beings separate and distinct from
what we now are ?   The philosopher who appealed from
Philip inflamed with wine to Philip in his hours of
sobriety, did not claim a judge so different as if he had
appealed from Philip in his youth to Philip in his old
age.   I cannot but be touched with the feeling so beauti-
fully expressed in a poem which I have heard repeated :—

> ' My eyes are dim with childish tears,
>     My heart is idly stirr'd,
> For the same sound is in my ears
>     Which in those days I heard.
> Thus fares it still in our decay,
>     And yet the wiser mind
> Mourns less for what age takes away
>     Than what it leaves behind.' " [1]

Sir Walter's memory, which, in spite of the slight
failure of brain and the mild illusions to which, on the
subject of his own prospects, he was now liable, had as yet
been little impaired—indeed, he could still quote whole
pages from all his favourite authors—must have recurred
to those favourite Wordsworthian lines of his with singular force, as, with Wordsworth for his companion, he
gazed on the refuge of the last Minstrel of his imagination
for the last time, and felt in himself how much of joy in
the sight, age had taken away, and how much, too, of
the habit of expecting it, it had unfortunately left behind.
Whether Sir Walter recalled this poem of Wordsworth's on
this occasion or not—and if he recalled it, his delight in
giving pleasure would assuredly have led him to let Wordsworth know that he recalled it—the mood it paints was
unquestionably that in which his last day at Abbotsford

[1] *The Antiquary*, chap. x.

was passed.  In the evening, referring to the journey
which was to begin the next day, he remarked that
Fielding and Smollett had been driven abroad by declining health, and that they had never returned; while
Wordsworth—willing perhaps to bring out a brighter
feature in the present picture—regretted that the last days
of those two great novelists had not been surrounded by
due marks of respect.  With Sir Walter, as he well knew,
it was different.  The Liberal Government that he had so
bitterly opposed were pressing on him signs of the honour
in which he was held, and a ship of his Majesty's navy
had been placed at his disposal to take him to the
Mediterranean.  And Wordsworth himself added his
own more durable token of reverence.  As long as English
poetry lives, Englishmen will know something of that
last day of the last Minstrel at Newark :—

> " Grave thoughts ruled wide on that sweet day,
>     Their dignity installing
> In gentle bosoms, while sere leaves
>     Were on the bough or falling ;
> But breezes play'd, and sunshine gleam'd
>     The forest to embolden,
> Redden'd the fiery hues, and shot
>     Transparence through the golden.
>
> " For busy thoughts the stream flow'd on
>     In foamy agitation ;
> And slept in many a crystal pool
>     For quiet contemplation :
> No public and no private care
>     The free-born mind enthralling,
> We made a day of happy hours,
>     Our happy days recalling.
>         *       *       *       *
> " And if, as Yarrow through the woods
>     And down the meadow ranging,
> Did meet us with unalter'd face,
>     Though we were changed and changing ;

If *then* some natural shadow spread
 Our inward prospect over,
The soul's deep valley was not slow
 Its brightness to recover.

" Eternal blessings on the Muse
 And her divine employment,
The blameless Muse who trains her sons
 For hope and calm enjoyment;
Albeit sickness lingering yet
 Has o'er their pillow brooded,
And care waylays their steps—a sprite
 Not easily eluded.
  *  *  *  *  *

" Nor deem that localized Romance
 Plays false with our affections ;
Unsanctifies our tears—made sport
 For fanciful dejections :
Ah, no ! the visions of the past
 Sustain the heart in feeling
Life as she is—our changeful Life
 With friends and kindred dealing.

" Bear witness ye, whose thoughts that day
 In Yarrow's groves were centred,
Who through the silent portal arch
 Of mouldering Newark enter'd ;
And clomb the winding stair that once
 Too timidly was mounted
By the last Minstrel—not the last !—
 Ere he his tale recounted."

Thus did the meditative poetry, the day of which was
not yet, do honour to itself in doing homage to the
Minstrel of romantic energy and martial enterprise, who,
with the school of poetry he loved, was passing away.

On the 23rd September Scott left Abbotsford, spending five days on his journey to London ; nor would he
allow any of the old objects of interest to be passed with-

out getting out of the carriage to see them. He did not
leave London for Portsmouth till the 23rd October, but
spent the intervening time in London, where he took medical advice, and with his old shrewdness wheeled his chair
into a dark corner during the physicians' absence from the
room to consult, that he might read their faces clearly on
their return without their being able to read his. They
recognized traces of brain disease, but Sir Walter was
relieved by their comparatively favourable opinion, for he
admitted that he had feared insanity, and therefore had
"feared *them*." On the 29th October he sailed for Malta,
and on the 20th November Sir Walter insisted on being
landed on a small volcanic island which had appeared four
months previously, and which disappeared again in a few
days, and on clambering about its crumbling lava, in spite
of sinking at nearly every step almost up to his knees, in
order that he might send a description of it to his old
friend Mr. Skene. On the 22nd November he reached
Malta, where he looked eagerly at the antiquities of the
place, for he still hoped to write a novel—and, indeed,
actually wrote one at Naples, which was never published,
called *The Siege of Malta*—on the subject of the Knights
of Malta, who had interested him so much in his youth.
From Malta Scott went to Naples, which he reached
on the 17th December, and where he found much
pleasure in the society of Sir William Gell, an invalid
like himself, but not one who, like himself, struggled
against the admission of his infirmities, and refused
to be carried when his own legs would not safely carry
him. Sir William Gell's dog delighted the old man; he
would pat it and call it "Poor boy!" and confide to
Sir William how he had at home "two very fine favourite
dogs, so large that I am always afraid they look too large

and too feudal for my diminished income." In all his
letters home he gave some injunction to Mr. Laidlaw
about the poor people and the dogs.

On the 22nd of March, 1832, Goethe died, an event
which made a great impression on Scott, who had intended
to visit Weimar on his way back, on purpose to see
Goethe, and this much increased his eager desire to
return home. Accordingly on the 16th of April, the last
day on which he made any entry in his diary, he
quitted Naples for Rome, where he stayed long enough
only to let his daughter see something of the place, and
hurried off homewards on the 21st of May. In Venice
he was still strong enough to insist on scrambling down
into the dungeons adjoining the Bridge of Sighs; and at
Frankfort he entered a bookseller's shop, when the man
brought out a lithograph of Abbotsford, and Scott remark-
ing, "I know that already, sir," left the shop unrecog-
nized, more than ever craving for home. At Nimeguen,
on the 9th of June, while in a steamboat on the Rhine,
he had his most serious attack of apoplexy, but would not
discontinue his journey, was lifted into an English steamboat at Rotterdam on the 11th of June, and arrived in
London on the 13th. There he recognized his children,
and appeared to expect immediate death, as he gave them
repeatedly his most solemn blessing, but for the most part
he lay at the St. James's Hotel, in Jermyn Street, without
any power to converse. There it was that Allan Cun-
ningham, on walking home one night, found a group of
working men at the corner of the street, who stopped him
and asked, "as if there was but one death-bed in London,
'Do you know, sir, if this is the street where he is
lying?'" According to the usual irony of destiny, it was
while the working men were doing him this hearty and

unconscious homage, that Sir Walter, whenever disturbed
by the noises of the street, imagined himself at the polling-
booth of Jedburgh, where the people had cried out, " Burk
Sir Walter." And it was while lying here,—only now
and then uttering a few words,—that Mr. Lockhart says
of him, " He expressed his will as determinedly as ever,
and expressed it with the same apt and good-natured
irony that he was wont to use."

Sir Walter's great and urgent desire was to return to
Abbotsford, and at last his physicians yielded. On the
7th July he was lifted into his carriage, followed by his
trembling and weeping daughters, and so taken to a
steamboat, where the captain gave up his private cabin—
a cabin on deck—for his use. He remained unconscious
of any change till after his arrival in Edinburgh, when,
on the 11th July, he was placed again in his carriage, and
remained in it quite unconscious during the first two
stages of the journey to Tweedside. But as the carriage
entered the valley of the Gala, he began to look about him.
Presently he murmured a name or two, " Gala water,
surely,—Buckholm,—Torwoodlee." When the outline
of the Eildon hills came in view, Scott's excitement was
great, and when his eye caught the towers of Abbotsford,
he sprang up with a cry of delight, and while the towers
remained in sight it took his physician, his son-in-law,
and his servant, to keep him in the carriage. Mr. Laidlaw
was waiting for him, and he met him with a cry, " Ha !
Willie Laidlaw ! O, man, how often I have thought of
you !" His dogs came round his chair and began to fawn
on him and lick his hands, while Sir Walter smiled or
sobbed over them. The next morning he was wheeled
about his garden, and on the following morning was out
in this way for a couple of hours ; within a day or two he

fancied that he could write again, but on taking the pen into
his hand, his fingers could not clasp it, and he sank back
with tears rolling down his cheek. Later, when Laidlaw said in his hearing that Sir Walter had had a little
repose, he replied, " No, Willie; no repose for Sir Walter
but in the grave." As the tears rushed from his eyes, his
old pride revived. " Friends," he said, " don't let me ex-
pose myself—get me to bed,—that is the only place."

After this Sir Walter never left his room. Occasionally
he dropped off into delirium, and the old painful memory,—
that cry of " Burk Sir Walter,"—might be again heard
on his lips. He lingered, however, till the 21st September,—more than two months from the day of his
reaching home, and a year from the day of Wordsworth's
arrival at Abbotsford before his departure for the Mediterranean, with only one clear interval of consciousness, on Monday, the 17th September. On that day Mr.
Lockhart was called to Sir Walter's bedside with the news
that he had awakened in a state of composure and consciousness, and wished to see him. " ' Lockhart,' he said,
' I may have but a minute to speak to you. My dear,
be a good man,—be virtuous,—be religious,—be a good
man. Nothing else will give you any comfort when you
come to lie here.' He paused, and I said, ' Shall I send
for Sophia and Anne?' ' No,' said he, ' don't disturb
them. Poor souls! I know they were up all night.
God bless you all!' " With this he sank into a very
tranquil sleep, and, indeed, he scarcely afterwards gave
any sign of consciousness except for an instant on the
arrival of his sons. And so four days afterwards, on the
day of the autumnal equinox in 1832, at half-past one in
the afternoon, on a glorious autumn day, with every
window wide open, and the ripple of the Tweed over its

pebbles distinctly audible in his room, he passed away,
and "his eldest son kissed and closed his eyes." He died
a month after completing his sixty-first year. Nearly
seven years earlier, on the 7th December, 1825, he had
in his diary taken a survey of his own health in relation
to the age reached by his father and other members of his
family, and had stated as the result of his considerations,
"Square the odds and good night, Sir Walter, about sixty.
I care not if I leave my name unstained and my family
property settled. *Sat est vixisse.*" Thus he lived just a
year—but a year of gradual death—beyond his own
calculation.

## CHAPTER XVII.

### THE END OF THE STRUGGLE.

SIR WALTER certainly left his "name unstained," unless
the serious mistakes natural to a sanguine temperament
such as his, are to be counted as stains upon his name;
and if they are, where among the sons of men would
you find many unstained names as noble as his with
such a stain upon it?   He was not only sensitively
honourable in motive, but, when he found what evil his
sanguine temper had worked, he used his gigantic powers
to repair it, as Samson used his great strength to repair
the mischief he had inadvertently done to Israel.  But with
all his exertions he had not, when death came upon him,
cleared off much more than half his obligations.   There
was still 54,000l. to pay.  But of this, 22,000l. was
secured in an insurance on his life, and there were besides
a thousand pounds or two in the hands of the trustees,
which had not been applied to the extinction of the debt.
Mr. Cadell, his publisher, accordingly advanced the
remaining 30,000l. on the security of Sir Walter's copyrights, and on the 21st February, 1833, the general
creditors were paid in full, and Mr. Cadell remained the
only creditor of the estate.   In February, 1847, Sir
Walter's son, the second baronet, died childless; and in
May, 1847, Mr. Cadell gave a discharge in full of all

claims, including the bond for 10,000*l.* executed by Sir
Walter during the struggles of Constable and Co. to
prevent a failure, on the transfer to him of all the copyrights of Sir Walter, including "the results of some
literary exertions of the sole surviving executor," which
I conjecture to mean the copyright of the admirable
biography of Sir Walter Scott in ten volumes, to which I
have made such a host of references—probably the most
perfect specimen of a biography rich in great materials,
which our language contains. And thus, nearly fifteen
years after Sir Walter's death, the debt which, within six
years, he had more than half discharged, was at last,
through the value of the copyrights he had left behind
him, finally extinguished, and the small estate of Abbotsford left cleared.

Sir Walter's effort to found a new house was even less
successful than the effort to endow it. His eldest son
died childless. In 1839 he went to Madras, as Lieutenant-
Colonel of the 15th Hussars, and subsequently commanded that regiment. He was as much beloved by the
officers of his regiment as his father had been by his own
friends, and was in every sense an accomplished soldier,
and one whose greatest anxiety it was to promote the welfare
of the privates as well as of the officers of his regiment.
He took great pains in founding a library for the soldiers
of his corps, and his only legacy out of his own family
was one of 100*l.* to this library. The cause of his death
was his having exposed himself rashly to the sun in a
tiger-hunt, in August, 1846 ; he never recovered from the
fever which was the immediate consequence. Ordered
home for his health, he died near the Cape of Good Hope,
on the 8th of February, 1847. His brother Charles died
before him. He was rising rapidly in the diplomatic

service, and was taken to Persia by Sir John MacNeill, on
a diplomatic mission, as attaché and private secretary.
But the climate struck him down, and he died at Teheran,
almost immediately on his arrival, on the 28th October,
1841. Both the sisters had died previously. Anne
Scott, the younger of the two, whose health had suffered
greatly during the prolonged anxiety of her father's illness,
died on the Midsummer-day of the year following her
father's death ; and Sophia, Mrs. Lockhart, died on the
17th May, 1837. Sir Walter's eldest grandchild, John
Hugh Lockhart, for whom the *Tales of a Grandfather*
were written, died before his grandfather ; indeed Sir
Walter heard of the child's death at Naples. The second
son, Walter Scott Lockhart Scott, a lieutenant in the
army, died at Versailles, on the 10th January, 1853.
Charlotte Harriet Jane Lockhart, who was married in
1847 to James Robert Hope-Scott, and succeeded to the
Abbotsford estate, died at Edinburgh, on the 26th
October, 1858, leaving three children, of whom only one
survives. Walter Michael and Margaret Anne Hope-
Scott both died in infancy. The only direct descendant,
therefore, of Sir Walter Scott, is now Mary Monica Hope-
Scott who was born on the 2nd October, 1852, the
grandchild of Mrs. Lockhart, and the great-grandchild of
the founder of Abbotsford.

There is something of irony in such a result of the
Herculean labours of Scott to found and endow a new
branch of the clan of Scott. When fifteen years after his
death the estate was at length freed from debt, all his own
children and the eldest of his grandchildren were dead ;
and now forty-six years have elapsed, and there only remains one girl of his descendants to borrow his name and
live in the halls of which he was so proud. And yet this,

and this only, was wanting to give something of the grandeur of tragedy to the end of Scott's great enterprise.   He
valued his works little compared with  the house and
lands which they were to be the means of gaining for his
descendants ; yet every end for which he struggled so
gallantly is all but lost, while his works have gained more
of added lustre from the losing battle which he fought so
long, than they could ever have gained from his success.

What there was in him of true grandeur could never
have been seen, had the fifth act of his life been less
tragic than it was.   Generous, large-hearted, and magnanimous as Scott was, there was something in the days
of his prosperity that fell short of what men need for their
highest ideal of a strong man.   Unbroken success, unrivalled popularity, imaginative effort flowing almost as
steadily as the current of a stream,—these are charac-
teristics, which, even when enhanced as they were in his
case, by the power to defy physical pain, and to live in
his imaginative world when his body was writhing in
torture, fail to touch the heroic point.   And there was
nothing in Scott, while he remained prosperous, to relieve
adequately the glare of triumphant prosperity.   His
religious and moral feeling, though strong and sound, was
purely regulative, and not always even regulative, where
his inward principle was not reflected in the opinions of
the society in which he lived.   The finer spiritual element in Scott was relatively deficient, and so the
strength of the natural man was almost too equal, complete, and glaring.   Something that should "tame
the glaring white" of that broad sunshine, was needed ;
and in the years of reverse, when one gift after
another was taken away, till at length what he called
even his "magic wand" was broken, and the old man

struggled on to the last, without bitterness, without
defiance, without murmuring, but not without such sudden flashes of subduing sweetness as melted away the
anger of the teacher of his childhood,—that something
seemed to be supplied. Till calamity came, Scott appeared to be a nearly complete natural man, and no
more. Then first was perceived in him something above
nature, something which could endure though every
end in life for which he had fought so boldly should
be defeated,—something which could endure and more
than endure, which could shoot a soft transparence of
its own through his years of darkness and decay. That
there was nothing very elevated in Scott's personal or
moral, or political or literary ends,—that he never for a
moment thought of himself as one who was bound to
leave the earth better than he found it,—that he never
seems to have so much as contemplated a social or political
reform for which he ought to contend,—that he lived to
some extent like a child blowing soap-bubbles, the brightest
and most gorgeous of which—the Abbotsford bubble—
vanished before his eyes, is not a take-off from the
charm of his career, but adds to it the very speciality of
its fascination. For it was his entire unconsciousness of
moral or spiritual efforts, the simple straightforward way
in which he laboured for ends of the most ordinary kind,
which made it clear how much greater the man was than
his ends, how great was the mind and character which
prosperity failed to display, but which became visible at
once so soon as the storm came down and the night fell.
Few men who battle avowedly for the right, battle for it
with the calm fortitude, the cheerful equanimity, with
which Scott battled to fulfil his engagements and to save
his family from ruin. He stood high amongst those—

> " Who ever with a frolic welcome took
>     The thunder and the sunshine, and opposed
>     Free hearts, free foreheads,"

among those who have been able to display—

> " One equal temper of heroic hearts
>     Made weak by time and fate, but strong in will,
>     To strive, to seek, to find, and not to yield."

And it was because the man was so much greater than the
ends for which he strove, that there is a sort of grandeur
in the tragic fate which denied them to him, and yet
exhibited to all the world the infinite superiority of the
striver himself to the toy he was thus passionately craving.

THE END.

N

For EU product safety concerns, contact us at Calle de José Abascal, 56–1°, 28003 Madrid, Spain or eugpsr@cambridge.org.

www.ingramcontent.com/pod-product-compliance
Ingram Content Group UK Ltd.
Pitfield, Milton Keynes, MK11 3LW, UK
UKHW012343130625
459647UK00009B/498